IN YARDS AND GARDENS

Books by Margaret Waring Buck

IN WOODS AND FIELDS

IN YARDS AND GARDENS

IN PONDS AND STREAMS

IN YARDS AND GARDENS

Written and illustrated by

MARGARET WARING BUCK

New York **ABINGDON PRESS** *Nashville*

FOR MARIE GAUDETTE
who suggested this book

THIS BOOK is for boys and girls and for all those who wish to know more about the living creatures and growing things in their yards and gardens. The book applies especially to the northeastern part of the United States, but nearly everything mentioned will also be found in other parts of the United States and in Canada. IN YARDS AND GARDENS is based on the author's year-round observation in her own yard and garden, supported by many field trips, much reading, and extensive study. Both manuscript and drawings were checked by specialists in the various fields included—birds, mammals, insects, plants, etc.

The author wishes to express her thanks and her indebtedness to Harold E. Anthony, Chairman and Curator, Department of Mammals, American Museum of Natural History; Richard H. Pough, Co-ordinator, Conservation and Use of Natural Resources, American Museum of Natural History; John Clare Pallister, Research Associate, Department of Insects and Spiders, American Museum of Natural History; William J. Clench, Research Associate, American Museum of Natural History and Curator of Mollusks, Museum of Comparative Zoology, Harvard College; Ted Pettit, Associate Editor, *Scouting Magazine,* Boy Scouts of America; Marie E. Gaudette, Nature Advisor, Program Department, Girl Scouts of U. S. A.; Dorothy Treat, National Audubon Society.

CONTENTS

IN YARDS AND GARDENS

You may live in the country and have open fields and woods around your yard or garden. You may live in a town where there are many small yards and gardens. Or you may live in the city and have a tiny yard surrounded by tall buildings. Wherever you live, you will find some wild creatures and growing things in the out-of-doors nearby. In the pages that follow you will learn what they look like and how they live.

BIRDS AND THEIR NESTS

Many birds come into our yards and gardens and some stay to build their nests. The ruby-throated hummingbird is more likely to come if we grow some deep-tubed red flowers such as petunias and bee balm. It may build its nest in a tree in a yard, although it is more likely to choose nearby woods.

This hummingbird is shiny green on the back and light underneath. The male has a crimson throat. Its bright coloring and tiny size (only 3½ inches long) and its food (tiny insects and the nectar of flowers) make it seem more like a butterfly than a bird.

The hummingbirds' nest is a small soft cup of down. It is covered with moss and lichens and fastened to the branch of a tree with spiders' webs. It is hard to find, as it looks like part of the tree.

The female lays two tiny eggs and sits on them for about two weeks. Then the eggs hatch into little birds that are no bigger than grasshoppers. The mother feeds them by putting her tongue or bill down their throats and pumping the baby birds full of a mixture of nectar and insects. In about three weeks the little birds are nearly as big as their parents.

RUBY-THROATED HUMMINGBIRD

ROBINS

BLUE JAYS

BIRDS THAT NEST IN TREES

Robins often like to live in our yards. Their bulky nest is easy to find. It is made of leaves and twigs on the outside. Inside it is covered with mud. The female robin shapes it into a cup by sitting in the mud and turning round and round. Then she adds some fine grass. Soon after, she lays four or five greenish-blue eggs. In about two weeks the eggs hatch. Both of the parent birds bring earthworms and insects to feed the young.

You have probably watched the robins in your yard turning their heads from side to side as they look or listen for worms. They cannot see directly in front of them, because their eyes are on the sides of their heads.

When the young birds are about two weeks old, they leave the nest. They continue to follow the parents around, begging to be fed, until they are almost full grown. The young robins have spotted breasts instead of plain red ones like their parents'.

If a blue jay builds a nest in your yard you will be wise not to go too close to it. The jay might swoop down and give you a swift peck on the head. The blue jay is a bold bird which has little fear of man or beast. Its bright blue, white, and black coloring makes it easy to see. It is a fairly large bird, about 11½ inches long. When it is annoyed or senses danger, it gives a hoarse call that can be heard at some distance.

Blue jays usually build their nests on a branch of a small tree near the trunk. They often choose evergreens. The nest is loosely made of sticks, leaves, and weed stems and is lined with strips of bark, grass, or other material. The female lays from three to six greenish-gray or brown-spotted buff eggs. Both the male and the female sit on the eggs until they hatch, in about seventeen days. Although the jays take good care of their own young, they sometimes destroy the eggs and young of smaller birds.

BIRDS THAT NEST IN SHRUBS

Catbirds often build their nests in snowball, lilac, or other bushes that they find in gardens. The nest in the picture was made of small hemlock twigs, grass, paper, string, and bits of chicken wire. It was lined with fine rootlets.

The female catbird lays from four to six glossy, greenish-blue eggs. The parents take turns sitting on the eggs for about two weeks, until they hatch. They raise one, two, or sometimes three families in a season. They feed the young birds insects. Later in the season the adult birds eat fruit and berries.

Catbirds are slate gray except for the top of the head, which is black, and a reddish-brown patch under the tail. They are about 9 inches long. The name comes from their catlike call. Their song is a medley of notes which often mimics other birds. If you have a birdbath in your yard you will probably have catbird visitors.

The brown thrasher is one of the most musical of our songbirds. Like the mockingbird and the catbird, it mimics other birds. It often gives a solo concert, perched on the top limb of a tree.

Thrashers, like thrushes, have bright brown on the back and a black-spotted light breast. They are larger than thrushes (about 11 inches long) and they have longer tails and a long bill that is slightly curved at the end.

The nest of the thrasher is built in a shrub or small tree, usually near the ground, or sometimes on it. The nest in the picture was in a pile of brush. It was made of twigs, paper, and leaves and was lined with rootlets.

The female thrasher lays from three to six eggs which are greenish-white, or buff speckled with reddish-brown. For two weeks, until the young birds hatch, one of the parents sits on the nest. One or two families are raised in a season. Thrashers eat fruit and insects.

CATBIRDS

BROWN THRASHER

CHIPPING SPARROW

SONG SPARROW

BIRDS THAT NEST IN SHRUBS OR VINES

Chipping and song sparrows are friendly little birds that often build their nests near houses. Sometimes they build in a vine growing over a porch or in a bush beside a doorway.

The chipping sparrow is smaller than the song sparrow; it is about 5½ inches long. It will attract your attention by the constant, cheerful chipping sound it makes as it hops around the yard. It is grayish-brown, streaked with black on the back and light underneath. The top of its head is brownish-red, and it has a black streak through the eye. The female is like the male but a little smaller, and the red patch on her head may be duller. In winter, which they usually spend in the southern states, both birds are duller in color.

In spring these sparrows build their nests in vines, bushes, or small trees. The nest is made of grass or fine roots lined with horsehair. The three to five eggs are bluish-green with dark spots. In a little less than two weeks the eggs hatch into young birds. The parents feed them small insects. When they are grown they will eat weed seeds as well as bugs.

The song sparrow is a little larger than the chipping sparrow. Both male and female are streaked with brown and black on the back. Underneath they are light with dark streaks, and there is a dark splotch in the center of the breast.

Some song sparrows remain in the north all winter. The others return from the south early in spring. You sometimes hear their sweet, trilling song on a warm day in February.

Song sparrows build their nests on the ground under a patch of grass, in a thick bush, or in a small tree. The nest is made of grass, weeds, and leaves and is lined with fine grass and hair. The three to five eggs are pale green with brown or lavender blotches. They hatch in about two weeks. After one family has been raised the female starts at once to lay more eggs. Sometimes she uses the same nest. There may be as many as three families in a season.

BIRDS THAT NEST IN HOLLOW TREES

The crested flycatcher builds its nest in a hollow tree or stump or in a birdhouse. It makes the nest of grass, rootlets, bits of bark, and sometimes hair and pine needles. It usually works a piece of cast-off snakeskin into the nest also. The female lays from four to six eggs which are cream colored with brown blotches and lines. The male and female take turns sitting on the eggs until they hatch, in about two weeks.

Flycatchers are olive colored on the back; brown and red on the wings and tail. On the throat they are gray. Underneath they are pale yellow. They are from 8½ to 9 inches long, the female being smaller than the male. Since they live on insects they are useful to have in the garden.

Screech owls live in hollow trees, in a woodpecker's deserted hole, or in a birdhouse. They do not make much of a nest. A few sticks, leaves, feathers, and bits of grass serve as a mattress for the eggs. Early in spring the female lays four or five white eggs, usually two or three days apart. She begins to set when she lays the first egg, and the eggs hatch three weeks or more after they are laid. So the young owls are different sizes.

At first the baby owls are covered with white down. This changes to a darker, heavier down before the feathers grow. The young owls stay in the nest for a month or more. Both parents feed them at night. When autumn comes, the young are marked like the adults.

Screech owls are mottled and streaked in brownish-gray or reddish-brown. There are some male and some female birds of each color. Both have feathered ear tufts. Screech owls are about 10 inches long. Unlike most other birds, the female is larger than the male. The large round eyes of the owl look straight ahead. To see at the side or in back, the owl can turn its head halfway around and look over its back.

The soft edges of the owls' feathers make it possible for them to fly silently. Owls live on frogs, insects, small birds, mice and other small animals.

CRESTED FLYCATCHER

SCREECH OWL

Flickers and other woodpeckers nest in hollows in trees. The flicker also lives in birdhouses and in holes in telephone poles. When it can, it returns to the same place every year. It does not like to make a new hole as its bill is not so strong as the woodpecker's. It is pointed rather than chisel-edged at the end. Its tongue is different also; it is smooth and sticky rather than barbed. This helps the flicker to catch the ants in the ground, which are its chief source of food.

The flicker is 12 inches or more long. It is brown and black with a red patch on the back of its head and white on the lower part of its back. The under side of the wings and tail is yellow. The male has a black cheek patch.

The male and female take turns sitting on the five, six, or more white eggs. When the young birds hatch, in about two weeks, both parents feed them on chewed-up ants.

The *rat-tat-tat* of a woodpecker's drilling is a familiar sound in spring. Woodpeckers are well fitted for digging out hollows in trees. They use their sharp-edged bills like chisels to cut out small chips. Their skulls are thick and hard. Their feet have two toes in front and two in back so they can get a good grip on the bark, and their tail feathers are so stiff that they can use them as a brace.

The hairy woodpecker is about 10 inches long. It is black and white, and the male has a red patch on the back of its head. We see these woodpeckers most often in winter. In summer they usually stay in the deep woods to raise their young, although sometimes they may choose an orchard tree. The female lays from three to six shiny white eggs. The parents take turns sitting on the eggs for about two weeks, until they hatch. The food of these birds is insects which they dig out of the bark, also ants, grasshoppers, and spiders.

FLICKER

HAIRY WOODPECKER

DOWNY WOODPECKER   WHITE-BREASTED NUTHATCH   BROWN CREEPER

The downy woodpecker is colored like the hairy woodpecker but is about 3 inches shorter. You may see one pecking insects out of the bark of a tree in your yard at any time of year. It chisels holes in dead trees for a sleeping place in winter and a nesting place in spring. The male bird makes the nesting hole. The female lays from four to six white eggs. The parents take turns sitting on them for about twelve days, until they hatch.

The woodpecker is useful in the garden, as it eats many insects. It can cut into the bark of a tree with its strong bill, and it can thrust its long tongue out beyond its bill. The tip of the tongue is hard and has many strong barbs with which to pull the insects out.

Another bird which eats insects in the bark is the white-breasted nuthatch. It cannot drill holes like the woodpecker but it can pick insects from the bark with its sharp bill. It can also climb around the trunk of a tree as easily with its head down as with it up. This is something the woodpecker, and most other birds, cannot do.

These nuthatches are gray, black, and white and are about 6 inches long. You may see them in your yard at any season of the year. They usually move about in pairs, and you will hear one calling to the other with a harsh *yank, yank*. They nest in spring in deserted woodpeckers' holes or other hollow places, or in a birdhouse. The female lays from five to eight eggs which are white or pinkish with brown spots. She sits on them for about two weeks, until they hatch.

Besides insects, these birds also eat soft-shelled nuts. They wedge the nuts into hollows in the bark to crack. This is the reason for the birds' name.

The brown creeper is a little smaller than the nuthatch. It is streaked brown and white on the back and is light underneath. Its sharp curved bill picks small insects and their eggs and cocoons out of the bark of trees. The creeper usually starts at the base of the tree and works up, going around the trunk, head up. We see it in winter as well as at nesting time in the spring. It often makes its nest in a fir tree in a hollow or under loose pieces of bark. The nest is made of twigs, bark strips, feathers, plant fibers, and cobwebs. The five to nine eggs which the female lays are white or creamy, spotted with brown or purple. She sits on the eggs for about two weeks, and she may raise two families in a season.

HOUSE WRENS

BIRDS THAT LIVE IN BIRDHOUSES

Some of the birds that nest in hollow trees will also make their homes in birdhouses that you set up in your yard. One of the liveliest and most friendly of these birds is the little brown-and-white house wren. Although it is only about 5 inches long, it bravely defends its nest against all enemies. If anyone comes near, it cocks its tail and sputters and scolds.

When not alarmed, the male wren has a sweet, bubbling song. He does not have so many home-making duties as the female, since he does not select the building place or build the nest. If Jenny Wren can find a birdhouse she uses it. Otherwise she makes her nest in any good sheltered spot. She builds it of small twigs and grass and lines it with soft plant down or feathers. Then she lays from six to eight white eggs with brown spots. For nearly two weeks she, and sometimes the male bird, sit on the eggs. After they hatch, the parents feed the young birds small insects until they are big enough to leave the nest.

A birdhouse for wrens should be about 8 inches deep. It should have a 1-inch hole 6 inches above the floor.

BLACK-CAPPED CHICKADEES

The black-capped chickadee is another little bird which will use a birdhouse. It is slightly larger than the wren and is black, gray, and white. It does not have the wren's quarrelsome disposition. All the year round we may hear its cheerful *chick-a-dee-dee* in our yards. It may not go south in winter as the wren and many other birds do. In spring, at nesting time, it has a sweet song that sounds like *phee-be*.

If the chickadee does not use a birdhouse it will nest in a hollow tree or where it has dug out the soft wood in a decayed tree. The nest is made of leaves and grass lined with moss, fur, or feathers. The female lays from four to eight brown-spotted white eggs. The parent birds take turns sitting on the eggs until they hatch, in a little less than two weeks. They may raise two families in a season.

The chickadees help the gardener by eating many insects, such as plant lice, bark beetles, spiders, flies, and ants. While searching for food in the bark of trees, these birds often cling to the branches upside down.

A birdhouse for chickadees should be fairly deep (to 12 inches) and should have a 1⅛-inch entrance hole 6 or 8 inches above the floor.

BLUEBIRD

Bluebirds are quick to take advantage of houses that are put up for their use. They often prefer them to their natural nesting places in hollow trees or posts. With their bright color and sweet song these birds make a delightful addition to any yard. They are bright blue on the back, rusty-brown on the breast, white underneath, and are about 7 inches long. When they return from the south, we know that spring is here.

A house for bluebirds may be made from a small hollow log, with each end covered and a 1½-inch hole bored in it for a door. It can be 8 or more inches deep, with the hole 6 inches above the floor. The log should be fastened to a tree or post from as high as you can reach, up to 30 feet.

The bluebirds' nest is made of grass, weed stalks, and bark, lined with fine grass. The female lays from four to six light blue eggs. She and the male take turns sitting on the eggs for twelve days, until they hatch. They may raise two or three families in a season. The young birds have speckled breasts like young robins.

These birds are not only pretty, but they are useful to have in the garden as they live almost entirely on insects and wild fruit.

PURPLE MARTIN

Purple martins will always nest in a birdhouse, if they can find one, rather than in their natural nesting place, a hole in a tree. They like a house with two or three floors and several compartments on each floor, so that a whole colony may live together. They will also nest in gourds with a hole bored in the side. The gourds may be hung from a pole with a bar extending from it.

Purple martins are the largest of the swallow family. They are about 8 inches long. The male is glossy blue-black all over. The female is gray underneath.

If you provide a house for the martins they will repay your hospitality by helping to rid your garden of insects such as boll weevils, squash bugs, moths, grasshoppers, dragonflies, flies, and mosquitoes. They will also drive crows and hawks from the neighborhood.

The martins' nest is made of mud on the outside, with grass, feathers, or any other suitable material on the inside. The female lays from four to six pure white eggs. She sits on them with little help from the male until they hatch, in about thirteen days. In the south two broods are raised in a season; in the north, only one.

BARN OWLS

BARN SWALLOWS AND NEST

BIRDS THAT NEST IN BUILDINGS

Some birds like to build their nests under the roofs of barns and abandoned buildings. The barn owl is one of these. It may nest in a hollow tree, but it is more likely to choose a building. Any kind of sheltered platform in a dark spot serves as a place to lay its eggs. If any nest at all is made, it consists only of a few sticks, hay, or trash. The female lays from five to eight or more white or yellowish eggs. She starts to sit on them as soon as the first egg is laid, and three weeks or so later the first one is hatched.

The young owls are downy and light colored, with the same odd, heart-shaped faces that the parents have. Sometimes they are called monkey-faced owls. Barn owls grow to 21 inches in length. The female is larger than the male. Both are light gray and buff in color. The feathers are beautifully marked in delicate black lines and spots.

Barn owls are useful about buildings as they destroy rats and mice. Their food consists of small animals and insects. Owls do their hunting at night. Their large, round eyes are able to see in the dark. They can see the movement of a field mouse in the grass, and their keen ears can hear it.

The barn swallow is another bird that makes its nest in barns. It prefers a barn that is near a small body of water, as it builds its nest of mud mixed with straw and grass. The nest is shaped like a bowl and is attached to the side of the building. The three to five eggs which the female lays are white, marked with red, brown, and lavender spots. The eggs hatch in about two weeks. Two or three families are raised in a summer. When the young are old enough to leave the nest, you may see them perched in a line on a roof or wire. There they wait for their parents to come and feed them.

Barn swallows are steel blue with a red patch on the forehead and throat. Underneath they are lighter red. They have deeply forked tails. The male is 7¾ inches long with a wingspread of 13½ inches. The female is a little smaller and is sometimes duller in color.

These swallows are useful, as they eat flies, mosquitoes, moths, wasps, and other insects. They catch their food as they fly. Often they skim over the surface of a pond to catch the insects that they find there.

NIGHTHAWK

HOMING PIGEON

BIRDS THAT NEST ON BUILDINGS

Some birds nest on, rather than in, buildings. A flat gravel-covered roof is often chosen by the nighthawk instead of its natural nesting place in an open field. The female lays her two eggs on the bare ground or roof. They are white with dark spots and blotches. The parents take turns sitting on the eggs from sixteen to nineteen days, until they hatch into down-covered babies.

The nighthawk is not a hawk. It belongs to the same family as the whippoorwill. This consists of medium-sized birds with long wings, small bills but deeply cleft mouths, weak feet, and mottled gray and brown coloring. The male nighthawk has a white throat, a white tail band, and a white patch on the wings. In the south it is called a bull bat because of its long wings and its habit of flying at night. Like a bat, it opens its mouth wide and catches insects as it flies.

If you should not have a chance for a close-up look at a nighthawk, you will know when one is in the neighborhood by the harsh, nasal call that it gives while flying. It also makes a booming sound when it dives and then starts upward again.

Homing pigeons nest on roofs, window sills, or other parts of buildings, either in the open, or in a dovecot or loft that has been prepared for them. We are all familiar with these birds which are found everywhere, in the city as well as around farmyards. They are about 15 inches long and are white or different shades of blue, gray, or red.

A pigeon usually keeps the same mate all its life. In April or May the female selects a nesting place for the first family of the season. The male brings some sticks or bits of rubbish to make a rough nest. Then the female lays two white eggs, about two days apart. The parents take turns sitting on the eggs for about seventeen days. They do not settle down, however, until after the second egg has been laid, so that the eggs will hatch at the same time. For the first five days the parents feed the young a cheesy milk that they pump up from their crops. After that, they feed them partly digested grain. When they are four weeks old the young are as big as the parents. After the young birds leave the nest, the parents raise a second family.

Pigeons may live as long as sixteen years.

BALTIMORE ORIOLE

The male oriole is orange and black. The female is yellow, brown, and black. Both are about 8 inches long. The basket-like nest hangs from the tip of a branch high in a tree. It is made of plant fibers, grass, hair, and string.

SCARLET TANAGER

The scarlet-and-black male is olive-yellow and black, like the female, in winter. Both are about 7 inches long. The nest is loosely built of stems, roots, and bark and is lined with rootlets. It is usually on a lower branch of a tree.

BLACK-AND-WHITE WARBLER

These little streaked black-and-white birds are about 5½ inches long. They creep around tree trunks, pecking at insects in the bark. Their bulky nest is made on the ground, of weeds, grass, and leaves, lined with hair.

YELLOW WARBLER

The yellow warbler is bright yellow, and the male has red streaks underneath. It is about 4¾ inches long. The nest is in a fork of branches in a shrub or small tree. It is made of plant fibers and strips of bark, lined with down and feathers.

AMERICAN GOLDFINCH

The male is yellow and black. In winter he is olive-yellow, brown, and grayish, like the female. Both are about 5 inches long. The nest, in a bush or small tree, is made of fine grass, bark strips, and moss, lined with thistledown.

RED-EYED VIREO

The vireo is greenish-gray above and white underneath. It is about 6½ inches long. The cup-shaped nest, in the fork of a low tree, is made of strips of bark, paper, and plant down, lined with fine bark strips and decorated with webs and bark.

WOOD THRUSH

This bright brown bird has a white breast spotted with black. It is about 8 inches long. The nest is made of leaves and twigs held together with mud and lined with fine roots and grass. Bits of paper or rag may be woven in it also.

ROSE-BREASTED GROSBEAK

The female is streaked brown and white. The male is black and white with a red throat. Both are about 8 inches long. The nest is in a low tree or bush. It is carelessly made of twigs, roots, and grass.

PHOEBE

These birds are greenish-gray on the back, light underneath, and are about 7 inches long. Their nest is usually built on a beam of wood or on a side wall. It is made of mud, grass, and plant fibers and is covered with moss.

ENGLISH SPARROW

These familiar birds are brown, streaked with black on the back, and light underneath. The male has a black throat; the female does not. The nest is usually made on the outer parts of buildings, of grass or other materials, lined with feathers.

CEDAR WAXWING

This neat bird is grayish-brown with black and has a yellow band on the tail. It is 7½ inches long. The rough nest, on a branch of a tree or bush, is made of bark, plant fibers, leaves, rootlets, paper, and twine, lined with finer materials.

TOWHEE or CHEWINK

The male is black and white with brownish-red on the sides. The female is more brownish. Both are about 8 inches long. Their nest, on the ground under bushes, is made of leaves, twigs, grass, and plant fibers, lined with grass and rootlets.

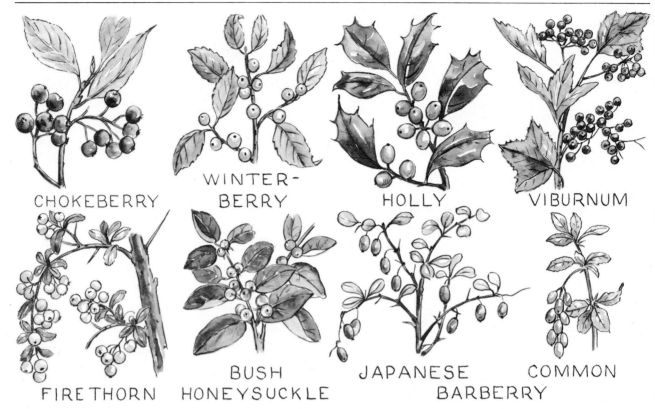

CHOKEBERRY WINTER-BERRY HOLLY VIBURNUM

FIRETHORN BUSH HONEYSUCKLE JAPANESE BARBERRY COMMON BARBERRY

SHRUBS WITH BERRIES

Birds come to gardens which have bushes or trees with berries. Why not plant some in your yard? The wild trees and shrubs may be moved from the woods when they are small. The cultivated kinds may be purchased from a nursery.

The chokeberry has clusters of small white and pink flowers in spring and red or black berries when its leaves turn red in autumn. It grows from 5 to 10 feet high.

The winterberry, or black alder, is a holly which drops its leaves in winter, leaving the clusters of coral berries on the stems. It grows wild in swampy places to a height of 20 feet. It may also be grown as a shrub in gardens.

Along the eastern coast and in the south holly grows as shrubs or small trees. It has shiny, thorny evergreen leaves. Only the female trees have the red berries.

Viburnums are bushes or small trees which have clusters of white flowers in spring and later have red berries which become bluish-black when ripe.

The various kinds have leaves of different shapes. The one in the picture has leaves like a maple. The nannyberry has smooth oval leaves, and the arrowwood has oval leaves with toothed edges. These three kinds of viburnums grow wild in the woods.

The tall, spreading, thorny stems of the fire thorn have clusters of small, oval evergreen leaves. In spring it has small white flowers. Late in summer dense clusters of bright orange berries form. They remain on the plant into the winter unless the birds strip them off.

Bush, or Tartarian, honeysuckles are large, spreading shrubs with many small red, white, yellow, or pink flowers in spring and red berries early in summer.

Barberries are eaten by game birds and some other birds. The two kinds of barberry bushes are easy to grow. The Japanese barberry makes a dense, thorny shrub about 4 feet high. It has many small red berries scattered along the stems. The common European kind grows to 8 feet high and has drooping clusters of red berries.

TREES WITH FLOWERS AND BERRIES

There are many small trees which you may plant to make your garden more beautiful and at the same time attract the birds. Most of these trees will grow where they are lightly shaded by other trees. But they will have a better shape if they are planted where they have room to spread out.

The mountain ash has flat-topped clusters of fragrant, white flowers in spring and orange berries in autumn. Its long leaves have from seven to fifteen leaflets. The native American ash grows to a height of 30 feet. The European kind, which is often planted in gardens, has larger berries and grows as high as 50 feet. Robins, starlings, and other birds like the berries.

Birds eat the white or bluish berries on the low-growing dogwoods, like the red osier, which has red stems and grows 10 feet high.

The bright red berries of the flowering dogwood are eaten by many birds. It is a pretty tree for a garden. In spring it is covered with large, showy white or pink flowers whose four petals (bracts, really) take the shape of a cross. In autumn, when the berries are ripe, the green leaves are mottled with scarlet.

The flowering crab apples are decorative small trees which have beautiful pink-and-white, fragrant flowers in spring and small apples in autumn. Cedar waxwings, grosbeaks, robins, and other birds like the apples.

The hawthorns, such as the scarlet haw, also have lovely flowers in spring and handsome fruits in autumn. They are small trees with stiff, thorny branches. The flowers are like clusters of single white or pinkish roses. The clusters of red fruit are like tiny apples.

Birds are so fond of the fruit of the mulberry tree that they seldom give it a chance to ripen. There are both wild and cultivated mulberry trees. Some have white fruit and some red. With their clean, shiny leaves they are attractive small trees. The paper mulberry, a native of Asia, will grow in city back yards as well as in country gardens.

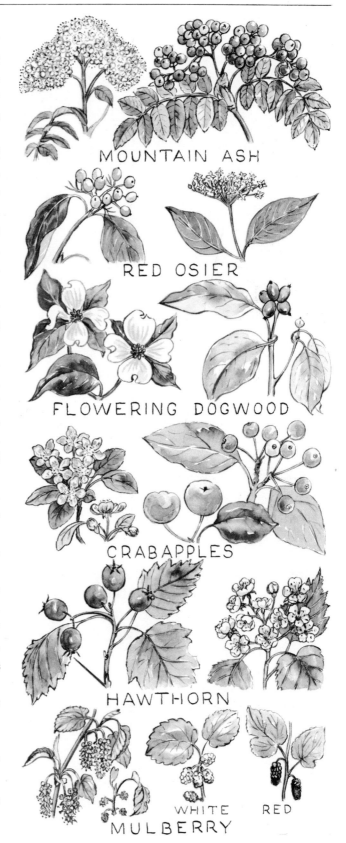

MOUNTAIN ASH

RED OSIER

FLOWERING DOGWOOD

CRABAPPLES

HAWTHORN

WHITE   RED
MULBERRY

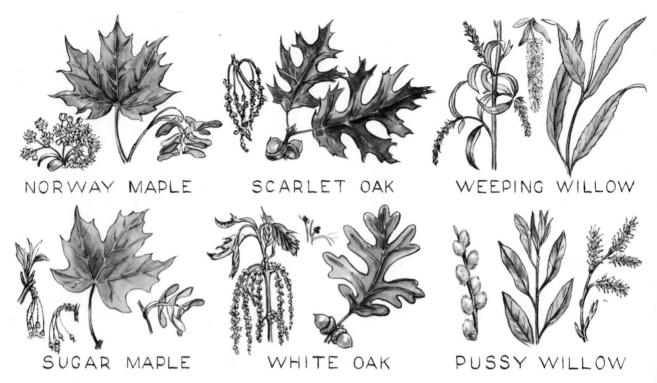

NORWAY MAPLE   SCARLET OAK   WEEPING WILLOW

SUGAR MAPLE   WHITE OAK   PUSSY WILLOW

SHADE TREES

You probably have in your yard some of the trees pictured here.

The Norway maple makes a compact, rounded tree, which grows to 100 feet high. The bark is dark gray and closely ridged. The leaves turn yellow in autumn. In early spring rounded clusters of yellow-green flowers cover the tree before the leaves are out. Winged seeds follow the flowers. Squirrels eat the buds and seeds of maple trees.

The sugar maple grows into a large tree about 135 feet high. Early in spring it may be tapped for its sap, which is boiled to make maple sirup and sugar. The tree has grayish bark with irregular ridges. Drooping clusters of tiny yellow flowers appear with the leaves.

The scarlet oak has bright red leaves in autumn. It is an irregular tree growing to 70 or 80 feet high. The deeply cut leaves have five to nine lobes and grow 6 inches long. The flowers are on slender catkins in spring, and the seeds are acorns.

The white oak grows to 150 feet high. It has light gray, ridged bark and gnarled branches. The leaves, which grow to 9 inches long, have five to seven rounded lobes. Dry leaves cling to the tree until late in winter. The flowers are in thin yellow catkins and small red clusters. They are followed by acorns. Squirrels plant many oak trees when they bury acorns and forget them.

The graceful weeping willow is a native of China. It prefers wet places but will grow on dry land also. The thick trunk has grayish bark divided into shallow ridges. Long, narrow leaves grow on long, thin, drooping branches. Broken branches root easily. New trees are started when the branches are carried by water to other places along the shore. The green flower catkins appear with the first leaves.

The familiar pussies on the pussy willow are budding catkins which have silvery tufts of hair between the scales. They come before the long narrow leaves which grow along the many upright branches. Try growing one of these small trees by sticking a pussy-willow branch into the ground. Choose a moist place if possible, though it will grow in dry land also.

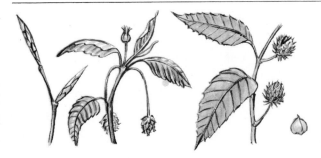

BEECH

The beech is a tall tree whose branches sometimes spread to the ground. The smooth bark is light gray. The flowers form in round heads on hanging stems and in small clusters when the leaves open. The seeds are nuts covered with burs.

POPLAR or COTTONWOOD

This quick-growing tree reaches 100 feet in height. The old bark is gray and deeply ridged; the young bark is greenish-yellow. The flowers are in long catkins and come before the leaves. The seeds form in long clusters in May.

SYCAMORE

You can tell this tree by its smooth white bark, mottled with greenish-brown, which peels off in patches. It grows to 170 feet high. The clustered flowers form balls in May. Seed balls hang from ropelike stems on the tree all winter.

AMERICAN ELM

Many of these tall, spreading trees grow along village streets. They have rough gray bark. The flowers form in small, drooping clusters before the leaves open. The clusters of flat seeds ripen when the leaves come.

WHITE ASH

The white ash grows into a very large tree with a thick trunk which has deeply ridged gray-brown bark. The flowers come before the leaves and look like bits of purple or green fringe. The small winged seeds hang in thick clusters.

GRAY BIRCH

The bark is chalky-white or grayish with triangular black patches under the branches. It is a short-lived tree which grows about 30 feet high. The flowers appear in catkins just before the leaves. The seeds are in conelike catkins.

SWEET CHERRY

PLUM

PEACH

PEAR

APPLE

FRUIT TREES

Fruit trees are both useful and decorative in the garden. Young trees purchased from a nursery are more satisfactory than any that you might grow from seed.

The sweet cherry is a large tree with smooth reddish-brown bark. It has long pointed leaves. The white flowers which come with the first leaves in April or May measure an inch or more across. The large yellow or red cherries ripen in early summer.

The sour cherry is a smaller tree and is easier to grow. Its white flowers come just before the leaves, and the round red fruits ripen early in summer.

Plum trees are grown mostly in the southern and western states but some kinds may be grown all over the United States. They form large, open trees with pointed oval leaves which grow to 4 inches long. The white or creamy fragrant flowers are 1 inch or less across and grow in small clusters. The flowers appear with the first leaves. The reddish, greenish-yellow, or purple fruits ripen in summer.

The peach is a native of China. It is a small, weak, rather short-lived tree with smooth, close brown bark. The limp leaves grow to 9 inches long and often fold together. The large flowered kind has handsome pink flowers about 2 inches across. Other kinds have smaller flowers. The flowers come before the leaves, in April or May. The velvety-skinned pink-and-yellow fruit is ready to pick in late summer.

The pear tree grows to 60 feet high. It has rough dark-colored bark and pointed oval leaves. The white flowers, about 2 inches across, grow in small clusters. The green or yellow fruit ripens late in summer.

Apple trees grow to 20 feet high and have spreading, twisting branches. The bark is rough and dark colored. The leaves grow to 4 inches long. The pink-and-white flowers, which are sometimes 3 inches across, come with the leaves in May. The red, yellow, or greenish fruit ripens from midsummer to frost.

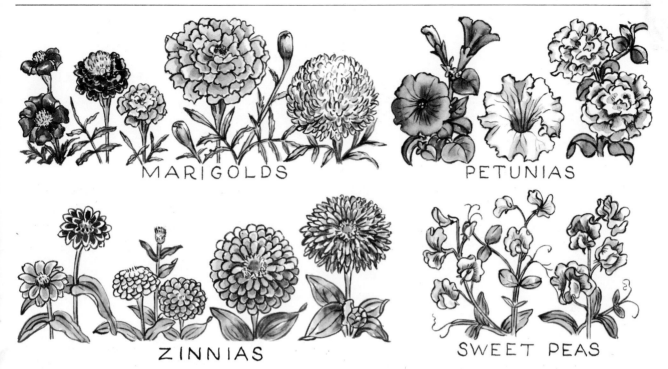

MARIGOLDS

PETUNIAS

ZINNIAS

SWEET PEAS

IMPROVED ANNUALS

Annuals grow from seeds planted in spring or the previous fall. They do not live through the winter. Many of the brightest and best-liked flowers in our gardens are annuals.

Seedsmen are working all the time to improve plants. They try to produce larger or differently shaped or colored flowers. Some flowers which grow in our gardens today are very different from those that grew in our grandparents' gardens.

Marigolds now come in many different sizes and shapes. There are carnation-flowered marigolds and chrysanthemum-flowered marigolds. The leaves of some kinds have lost the spicy marigold odor. Giant marigolds grow to 3 feet high and often have flowers over 4 inches across. Dwarf marigolds are only 1 foot tall; they have single or double flowers. All of the blossoms are in shades of yellow, orange, or red. If you plant the seeds in spring in good soil in a sunny location the dwarf kinds will start to bloom early in summer. The taller kinds bloom from midsummer to frost.

Zinnias have a wide range of colors as well as of sizes and shapes. They come in cream, white, and many shades of yellow, orange, red, and purple. There are dahlia-flowered zinnias and some with curled petals. The giant kinds grow to 3 feet high and have flowers 5 or 6 inches across. The miniature and pompon kinds are 1 foot tall with 1-inch flowers. Zinnia seeds should be planted in spring in fairly good soil, though some kinds will thrive in poor soil. The flowers bloom all summer.

Petunias bloom all summer. The flowers are white and shades of red, blue, and purple. Single petunias are as large as 4 inches across. There are also giant fringed, ruffled, and double varieties. The seeds of the large flowering and double petunias should be started indoors early in spring. The seeds of the smaller petunias may be sown outdoors as soon as the ground is warm.

The old-fashioned sweet pea has been developed into large flowering varieties with long stems. Some kinds have waved and ruffled flowers. They are white, cream, and many shades and combinations of blue, rose, lavender, and orange. Sweet-pea seeds should be planted early in spring in rich soil in specially prepared trenches. The vines, which grow to 6 feet high, need a support.

CANDYTUFT

These plants grow from 6 to 12 inches tall and are covered with clusters of white, pink, or lavender blossoms. If you make several sowings of seeds you will have flowers all summer. Candytuft likes a sunny location.

VERBENA

This is a trailing plant that grows well in a light soil in a sunny place. The red, white, blue, or purple flowers bloom from midsummer until fall. The dwarf kinds are good for borders; the tall kinds grow to 18 inches high.

SWEET ALYSSUM

This makes a good border plant as it grows to only 4 inches high. The clusters of tiny white or purple flowers are fragrant and bloom all summer. Alyssum is easily grown in almost any kind of soil in a sunny place.

PORTULACA

This is also called sun plant as it thrives in dry, sandy soil in sunny locations. The seeds are fine and may be mixed with sand before sowing. The single or double flowers come in shades of red, orange, yellow, and white.

ANNUAL PHLOX

These flowers come in many shades of red and lavender, also in creamy yellow and white. They bloom all summer in a sunny place and are good for cutting. Phlox plants grow from 10 to 20 inches high, depending on the variety.

ANNUAL PINKS

These flowers come in both single and double varieties in many combinations of red, pink, and white. Seeds sown in spring will grow to 1 foot high in a sunny place. They will bloom in summer. Some plants may live through the winter.

CORNFLOWER or BACHELOR'S BUTTON

These flowers — blue, white, pink, or red — come into bloom a few weeks after the seed is sown. They will bloom all summer if the faded flowers are picked. The dwarf kinds are 1 foot tall; others grow to from 2 to 2½ feet high.

NASTURTIUMS

These bright flowers grow well in poor soil in a sunny spot. There are dwarf and climbing varieties. The single or double flowers bloom all summer. They come in shades of yellow, orange, and red. Soak the seeds overnight and plant in spring.

POPPIES

There are several kinds of annual poppies that are easy to grow in sunny places — 1) Shirley; 2) carnation; 3) California. The fine seeds should be sown where they are to grow as the plants should not be transplanted.

COSMOS

The tall-growing cosmos blooms in summer and autumn. It likes light soil and a sunny place. The flowers are usually pink, white, and crimson. One variety is yellow, and one late-flowering kind is double.

LARKSPUR

The white, blue, purple, or pink flowers come in single or double varieties. Larkspur grows to about 3 feet tall. It blooms all summer and is good for cutting. The seed should be sown in a sunny spot early in spring.

SUNFLOWERS

The miniature sunflower grows to 4 feet tall and has many blossoms in shades of yellow or red. The flowers are single or double. The giant sunflower grows to 10 feet tall and blooms in summer and fall. Birds like its seeds.

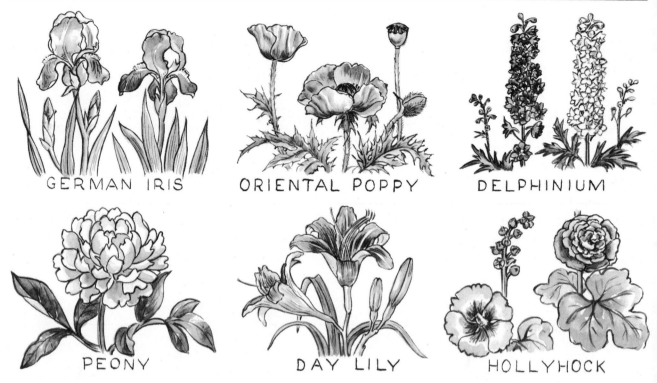

GERMAN IRIS — ORIENTAL POPPY — DELPHINIUM

PEONY — DAY LILY — HOLLYHOCK

PERENNIALS

Perennial plants have roots that live through the winter. Usually they live for many years. You may buy the plants from a nursery. Or you may grow them from seeds. Then they will have leaves the first year. The second year they will bloom. The tender varieties will need some protection through the first winter.

A favorite perennial is the iris. There are many different kinds. The German, or bearded, iris pictured here has large flowers in many shades of pink, purple, yellow, and white. The plants grow to 3 feet tall and have long, stiff, pointed leaves. The Siberian iris has narrower leaves and smaller flowers. The Japanese iris has large flat flowers. There are also low-growing kinds which bloom early in spring. All kinds of iris like rich, well-drained soil in sun or partial shade.

The peony blooms in May and June. Its showy double blossoms in white, pink, or red, grow as large as 6 inches across. There is also a single variety. Peony plants grow to about 3 feet tall. They like rich soil and a sunny place.

The Oriental poppy blooms in May or June. It has large pink, red, or white flowers that are black near the center. The plants grow from 3 to 4 feet tall and have coarse, hairy, deeply cut leaves. They are easily grown in good soil in a sunny place.

Day lilies bloom over a period of several months. The different varieties come in many shades of yellow, orange, and red. The orange lily, which blooms in May and June, is often found growing wild. It grows to 4 or more feet tall in rich or poor soil, in sun or shade.

Delphinium is the perennial larkspur. Its flowers grow in long spikes on stems up to 4 feet high. It blooms in June in shades of blue, pink, purple, and white. If the flowers are not allowed to go to seed, they will bloom again later in the summer. The plants like deep, rich, well-drained soil in a sunny place.

Hollyhocks have either double or single flowers in shades of red, pink, yellow, and white. They bloom in summer on tall stalks that grow from 5 to 6 feet high. They grow best in a sunny place and should be planted against a support.

1) PANSY; 2) VIOLA

Pansies may be started from seeds or bought from a nursery. Violas, which have smaller flowers in shades of blue, apricot, yellow, red, and white, are hardier and will live for a number of years. Faded blossoms should be removed.

PRIMROSE: 1) PRIMULA; 2) EVENING

The early-blooming primroses (Primula) come in many shades of yellow, red, and blue. They like partial shade and grow from 6 to 9 inches tall. The evening primroses bloom in summer. They have yellow, pink, or white flowers and grow taller.

1) COREOPSIS; 2) GAILLARDIA

Coreopsis has single or double golden-yellow flowers. Gaillardia, or blanket flower, has yellow-and-red daisy-like flowers. Both bloom all summer and are easy to grow in sunny, dry places. They grow to about 2 feet tall and are good for cutting.

PHLOX

The clustered flowers of phlox bloom all summer in shades of red, blue, violet, and white. The tall varieties grow to 4 feet high and make showy garden plants. They like plenty of sun and should not be allowed to become crowded.

FALL ASTER or MICHAELMAS DAISY

Varieties of this aster grow from 6 inches to 6 feet tall. The blue, purple, pink, or white clusters of small daisy-like flowers bloom from late summer through the fall. The wild kinds may be brought from fields and planted in the garden.

CHRYSANTHEMUMS

These flowers bloom in the fall. They come in many sizes, from the tiny pompons to the giant blooms of the florists. The colors are shades of pink, yellow, red, bronze, and white. One kind, the azaleamum, blooms all summer.

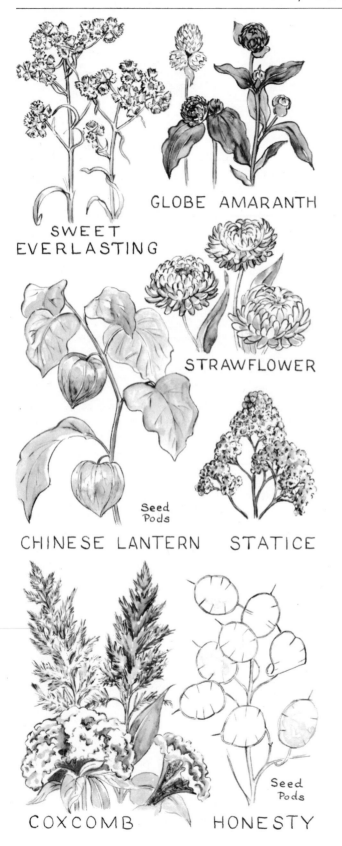

GLOBE AMARANTH

SWEET
EVERLASTING

STRAWFLOWER

Seed
Pods

CHINESE LANTERN   STATICE

COXCOMB   HONESTY

Seed
Pods

EVERLASTINGS

Some flowers will last for a long time after they have been picked and dried. It is fun to grow them in the garden and keep them for winter bouquets. Cut the flowers before they are open wide, strip off the leaves. Then tie the stems together with a piece of string, and hang them upside down in a dry place until they are stiff.

Pearly everlasting and sweet everlasting are found in fields. They have clusters of small white flowers with rows of tiny paper-like petals and gray-green woolly leaves. Try planting some in a sunny spot in your garden. They will live for years and will bloom from July to October.

The globe amaranth has rounded flower heads, like a clover, which come in shades of red, orange, and white. Plant the seeds in your garden in the spring and they will start to bloom in midsummer.

Strawflowers come in bright colors which last after the flower is dried. The flowers grow to 2½ inches across. They bloom from midsummer until late fall from seeds that are sown in spring. The stems of the dried flowers usually have to be wired.

Chinese lantern plants have bright orange-red seed pods which remain on the stem after it is cut and dried. The "lanterns" come the second year after the seeds are planted.

Statice has clusters of small yellow, rose, blue, or white flowers which last a long time. Sow the seeds in spring, and the flowers will bloom in summer.

Coxcomb, or celosia, has plumelike or rounded flower heads which are showy in the garden and also in winter bouquets. They come in shades of bright crimson and yellow. The plants grow from 1 to 3 feet high. The seeds should be sown in rich soil in the spring.

The honesty plant blooms the second year after the seed is started. The round, flat seed pods follow the magenta-colored flowers which come early in spring. Remove the outer brown skin of the seed pods and you will have the "silver shillings" that are used for winter decoration.

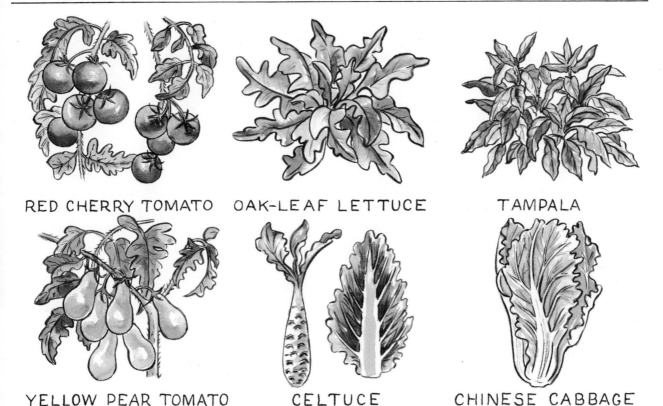

RED CHERRY TOMATO   OAK-LEAF LETTUCE   TAMPALA

YELLOW PEAR TOMATO   CELTUCE   CHINESE CABBAGE

UNUSUAL VEGETABLES

Seed growers keep improving the size, taste, and quality of vegetables. They have been able to grow varieties strong enough to resist many of the plant diseases and they have found ways of producing new kinds of vegetables.

People used to think tomatoes were poisonous. They grew them in flower gardens as decorative plants. Now tomatoes are one of the most popular garden vegetables. Some kinds have fruits that weigh as much as a pound. Some have small red fruits like cherries; others have small yellow fruits shaped like pears or plums. All kinds of tomato plants should be grown where they will get sunlight all day. Give each plant plenty of room to spread out and some kind of support. You may purchase small plants from the florist to set out when danger of frost is past. Or you may start seeds in a flat box of earth in the house very early in spring.

Lettuce comes in many different forms. The kind which has indented leaves is called oak-leaf lettuce. Celtuce is a kind of lettuce which has thick stems through the center of its leaves. These stems are cooked and eaten like celery. Iceberg lettuce forms a solid, crisp head. Boston lettuce makes a looser head; romaine a taller head. *(See page 36.)*

Tampala is a green that is grown and cooked like spinach. It has been used in China and India for centuries but only recently has it been grown in this country. Some kinds have light or dark green leaves, and one kind has green and red leaves. Tampala likes hot weather, so do not plant the seeds until the ground is warm. Plant it in a sunny spot. In six to eight weeks the leaves will be ready.

Chinese, or celery, cabbage is a cool-weather vegetable which may be shredded and used in salads or cooked like cabbage. The seeds should be sown very early in spring where summers are cool. Or they may be started in August for a late fall crop. The crisp, ruffled, pale green or white leaves grow from 12 to 18 inches tall.

CUCUMBER

Plant when danger of frost is past and again four weeks later. Sow seeds in groups 4 or 5 feet apart and thin the plants to four or five in a group. Vines may trail on the ground or climb on a fence. Cucumbers are ready to pick in about two months.

SPINACH

Sow seeds early in spring and cover with 1 inch of soil. Other sowings may be made later in spring and late in summer. Thin the plants to stand 6 inches apart in rows about 2 feet apart. The spinach is ready to use in about a month and a half.

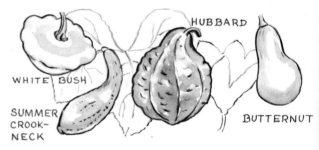

SWISS CHARD

Sow seed in rows about 2 feet apart any time from early spring to midsummer. Cover with ½ inch of soil. Thin the plants to 10 inches apart. The greens, both leaves and stems, will be ready to cook in two months or less.

SQUASH

Sow seeds after danger of frost is past, in small hills, about five to a hill. Allow 4 feet between hills for bush, and 8 feet for crookneck. Summer squash matures in two months or less; winter squash (Hubbard and butternut) in three months or more.

SWEET CORN

Plant seeds when ground is warm. Sow them several inches apart, in rows with 2 or 3 feet between them. Cover with 1 inch of soil. You may want to plant both early and late varieties. The ears ripen in three months or less.

LETTUCE

Sow seeds in rich soil early in spring and late in summer, as lettuce grows best in cool weather. Plant in rows 1½ feet apart and thin the plants to 1 foot apart. Loose leaf lettuce is ready in less than two months; head lettuce, in eighty days.

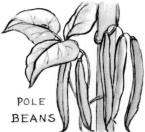

STRING BEANS

Plant seeds when soil is warm. Plant bush beans in rows about 2 feet apart, with 6 inches between plants. Pole beans climb on poles placed 4 feet apart, five or six plants to each pole. Bush beans mature in fifty days; pole beans, in sixty-five.

CABBAGE

Sow seeds in spring in deep, rich, well-drained soil. Thin or transplant to allow 18 to 24 inches between plants. The hard, rounded heads will be ready to use in two or three months, depending on whether early or late varieties are planted.

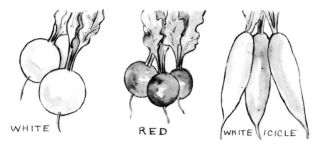

CARROTS

Sow seeds thinly in early spring in rows 1 foot apart. Thin the young plants to leave 3 inches between them. Another sowing may be made for a later crop. In two and a half months or less carrots will be ready to eat.

RADISHES

Sow seeds in early spring and again later in spring and late in summer. Plant in rows about 1 foot apart and cover with ½ inch of soil. Thin to 1 or 2 inches apart. Radishes grow best in cool weather and are ready in three or four weeks.

BROCCOLI

Sow seeds in spring in rows 2½ feet apart and thin the plants to stand about 18 inches apart. The budded flower heads form in late summer and early fall. They should be cut before the flowers open. After center head is cut, side buds form.

BEETS

Sow seeds early in spring and again later for a second crop. Space rows about 1½ feet apart and thin the plants to 2 or 3 inches apart. The roots will be ready to use in about two months. The tops may be used as greens earlier.

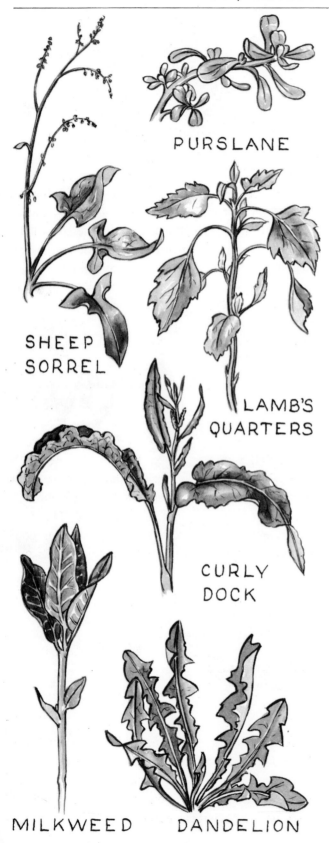

PURSLANE

SHEEP SORREL

LAMB'S QUARTERS

CURLY DOCK

MILKWEED   DANDELION

WEEDS THAT ARE GOOD TO EAT

Growing wild in your yard you will probably find several kinds of green plants that are good to eat. They may be eaten raw in salads or they may be cooked as greens.

Sheep sorrel grows in waste places all over the United States. It came from Europe originally. The green leaves are shaped like arrowheads and grow on long stalks. They have a sour taste when eaten raw. Sorrel leaves are good in a salad. They may also be cooked.

Purslane, or pussley, is a sprawling plant with fleshy green leaves tinged with red. The smooth thick stem is green or reddish and is easily broken. Purslane is a native of Europe and the southwestern United States. It grows wild in dooryards and waste places. The leaves may be eaten raw or they may be boiled.

The leaves of lamb's-quarters, or pigweed, may be cooked like spinach. The young leaves may be eaten raw. The seeds which form along the stems late in summer also may be eaten raw, or they may be dried and cooked as a cereal. The plants originally came from Europe and Asia, but lamb's-quarters is now a common weed throughout the United States and Canada. It grows to 3 feet high, and the leaves are smooth and frosty green.

Curly dock, or yellow dock, has long, wavy leaves on a thick stem that grows to 3 feet high. The rosette of leaves at the base of the stem is the part that is eaten in spring and autumn. The leaves are cooked as greens.

The young milkweed shoots that appear in spring and early summer may be eaten raw or cooked as greens. When the plant is fully grown the stout, partly fuzzy stem has milky juice in it. It grows to 5 feet high. The leaves are dark green on top and light underneath, with thick veins.

The dandelion's deeply cut leaves form a rosette from which the yellow flowers and downy seed balls rise on hollow stems. In spring the leaves are used as a green, either raw or boiled. They may be combined with other greens in a salad.

BUMBLEBEE
with pollen
basket full

HONEYBEES

BEES

Bumblebees gather nectar and pollen from the flowers in our gardens. The nectar, they suck through their long tongues. The pollen, they collect in a wide section of their hind legs, called the pollen basket.

The bumblebee's home is in a hole in the ground. It is started in the spring by the queen bee, as the other bees do not live through the winter. She either finds a hole ready-made or digs one in loose soil. Then she gathers some nectar and pollen and makes it into a paste inside the hole. She lays her eggs on the paste.

The grubs (larvae) which hatch from the eggs eat it. When the grubs are full grown they spin cocoons and form pupas inside. Then they change into worker bees. The workers take over the task of feeding the new grubs which hatch from the next batch of eggs that the queen lays. The workers also enlarge the nest and make waxen cells.

Late in summer male and female bees are raised. They mate, and the females become queens. When cold weather comes, the male and worker bees die. The queens hibernate until spring. Then they start new nests.

Bumblebees are from ½ to 1 inch long. They have heavy, velvety, black-and-yellow bodies. There are a number of different kinds. Some have more black and others more yellow on their bodies. At the end of the body is a stinger. It does not pull out when the bee stings, as a honeybee's stinger does. So the same bumblebee may sting you more than once!

Honeybees came from Europe originally, but they are now found all over the United States. They have black-and-golden rings on the lower part of their bodies. They are smaller and thinner than the bumblebees.

Honeybees make their homes in hives or in hollow places in trees or other shelters. Like the bumblebees, they live in colonies which consist of a queen and workers. When one home becomes too crowded, a new queen is raised. Then the old queen, with some of the workers, finds another place to live. The workers build a comb from wax that forms on the under side of their bodies. The comb has many cells. The queen lays her eggs in some; in others, the workers store the honey and pollen that is needed for food in winter.

The same comb is used year after year. The bees repair it when necessary. When a new queen is to be raised, a larger cell is made. A grub hatches from the egg which is laid in that cell. It is fed a special kind of food called royal jelly. Queen bees may live for several years. Worker bees live only a few weeks in the active summer season, but they may live several months through the winter.

Honeybees are useful for the honey that they make and because, like the bumblebees, they carry pollen. Pollen must be carried from one plant to another before seeds can be formed.

PAPER WASP   POTTER WASP   MUD DAUBER

WASPS AND HORNETS

Hanging from the eaves or from trees you may find a wasp nest or a hornet nest. The paper-wasp's nest has a single row of cells that are open underneath. It is fastened to a support by a stem at the top. The grubs (larvae) hatch from eggs which are laid in the cells. They hang head downward and are fed from below. Paper wasps (Polistes) have slender, dark bodies about ¾ of an inch long.

Potter wasps make rounded nests, like little clay jugs, which they attach to a support. Each nest has only one cell. The wasp puts caterpillars in it for the grub to eat. These wasps are dark with yellow rings on their bodies and are about ½ inch long.

The mud dauber's nest is a layer of tube-shaped cells covered with mud. The female places paralyzed spiders in the cells to feed the grubs. Mud daubers have long, thin waists. One kind is black and brown and has orange legs. Another kind is steel blue. The blue kind uses the nest of the black-and-brown mud dauber. After clearing out the cells, she places her own eggs and spiders inside.

Hornet colonies have queens and workers. Only the young queens live through the winter. In spring each one makes a small nest of a few cells. In each cell she lays an egg. The egg hatches into a grub which the queen feeds on chewed-up insects. These grubs become worker hornets. They feed the new grubs and add more cells to the nest. Later, males and females hatch from the eggs.

The white-faced hornets have a large, cone-shaped paper nest. You have probably seen one hanging from a beam, branch, or other support. It may be the home of thousands of hornets. It is not wise to disturb them as they are quick to sting. The white-faced hornet is black with white marks and is an inch or so long. The giant hornet, which came from Europe, is a little over an inch long and is brown and yellow. Its paper nest is made in sheltered places, often in buildings or hollow trees.

Yellow jackets are black and yellow or black and white. They are about ¾ of an inch long. Their nest of paper cells is in an underground hole or other shelter.

WHITE-FACED HORNET

GIANT HORNET

YELLOW JACKETS

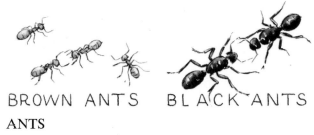

BROWN ANTS   BLACK ANTS

ANTS

If you turn over a large stone in your yard you may uncover a city of ants. In lifting the stone, you are taking the roof off their underground home. The ants will race about and dart down their tunnels. The worker ants will carry the eggs, grubs, and cocoons to safety deeper in the earth. The queen, an oversized ant, may be down in a tunnel where you cannot see her.

An ant city, like a colony of bees, is started by a queen. She digs a hole in the ground and stops up the opening with some dirt. Then she begins to lay eggs. The eggs hatch into small, fat grubs which the queen feeds with her oily spittle. When the grubs are full grown they spin cocoons and change into worker ants. They push the dirt away from their doorway and start out to find food. They bring some back to the queen. She lays more eggs which hatch into grubs. Then the worker ants bring food to the grubs.

Ants live on liquid food. They suck the juices from other insects and they collect the honeydew that aphids (plant lice) give off. A food-gathering ant has two stomachs — one for its own use and one in which it stores food for the other ants. It passes the drops of food from its mouth to the mouth of another ant.

All of the workers do not go out hunting for food. Some stay at home and look after the grubs.

EGGS   GRUBS   COCOONS   ANTS

Some take care of the queen. Some keep the city clean. And some act as soldiers to protect the city. Later in the season male and female ants are hatched. They have wings and they fly to find mates. Then the males die and the females fly off to start new colonies.

All ants do not live under stones. Some, like the big black carpenter ants, get into houses and make tunnels through the wood. Little red ants also live in houses. Small brown ants live in fields.

If you wish to see how the ants live, you may raise a colony in a shallow plaster box with a glass over the top, or in a glass ant house, or even in a bottle. Put some soil in the place where you want to keep the ants. Then hunt for a queen ant, some workers, and cocoons. Put them on the soil and cover the container tightly so they cannot escape. Feed them sugar or honey and water and bits of meat and fruit.

To make a glass ant house, fasten together three sides of a narrow wooden frame. Bore two holes in the top of the frame and put removable covers over the holes. (You can drop food to the ants through them.) Get two pieces of glass to fit the frame. Fasten them to the outside of it with adhesive tape. Fill the space between the pieces of glass with earth to within ½ inch of the top. Then put in the ants and fasten the top of the frame on with tape.

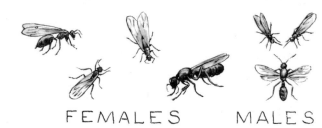

FEMALES   MALES
ANTS WITH WINGS

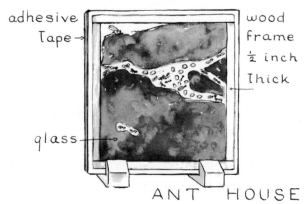

adhesive Tape →

wood Frame ½ inch Thick

glass →

ANT HOUSE

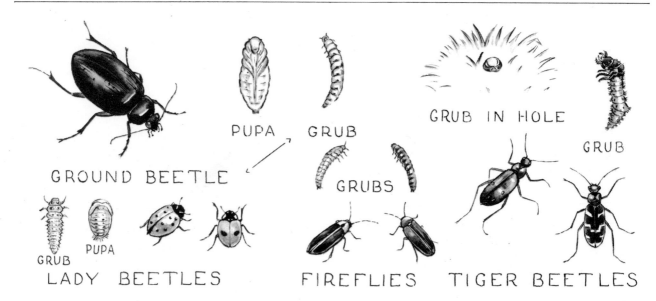

PUPA GRUB

GROUND BEETLE

GRUB IN HOLE

GRUB

GRUBS

GRUB

LADY BEETLES FIREFLIES TIGER BEETLES

PUPA

BEETLES

There are thousands of different kinds of beetles in the United States. You will probably find many in your yard. Some beetles are useful, as they eat harmful insects. Other beetles cause damage by eating plants.

Beetles go through four forms of life. First come the eggs which the female lays in the ground or on plants. The eggs hatch into grubs (larvae). These later change into pupas. The pupas turn into adult beetles.

You can tell beetles from other insects by the hard outer (fore) wings which cover most of their body when they are quiet. When they fly, they spread their outer wings and use the filmy under (hind) wings to propel them through the air.

Ground beetles are usually plain black or brown, although some kinds are marked with bright colors. They vary in size from less than ½ inch to 1¼ inches long. They eat other insects, including caterpillars. Most of them hunt for food at night. During the day they hide under stones or other cover. Sometimes you can catch these beetles by sinking in the ground a bottle or can with a little molasses in it.

Lady beetles are useful in the garden in both grub and adult forms, as they live on aphids. One grub may eat as many as fifty aphids in a day.

There are several kinds of lady beetles. They are all small, about ¼ inch long, with a fat shape, but they differ in color and in the number of spots. Some are red or yellow with black spots; some are black with red or yellow spots.

Fireflies are narrow, flat beetles, ½ to ⅝ of an inch long. On the back they are brown or gray with light lines. The spot that lights up is at the end of the body. The light flashes at regular intervals and is a signal by which the fireflies attract each other. Some of the grubs are luminous. So are the wingless females of some species of fireflies. These are glowworms. Fireflies eat worms, snails, slugs, and sometimes plants.

Tiger beetles are slender, active creatures which eat other insects. One kind that is often seen in yards is a beautiful bright blue-green color. It is about ½ inch long. Others are shiny green or purple with interesting patterns on the back. The females lay eggs in the ground. The grubs which hatch from the eggs live in holes in the ground. When the grub wants something to eat, it sticks its large, broad head out of the top of the hole and waits to grab a passing insect. A hump on its back helps it to brace itself against the sides of the hole while it reaches out. The grub changes into a pupa inside the hole. And the pupa becomes a tiger beetle.

Click beetles are mostly black or brownish, and are medium or small in size. They have a hinge on their bodies at the base of the wings. When they fall or are laid on their backs, they are able to bend their bodies, then straighten out with a snap that sends them into the air. The grubs of these beetles are long, thin, round wireworms with hard brown or yellow skins. Some live in the ground and eat plant roots; some live in dead wood or decaying leaves, or under bark. Some eat other insects. The wireworms may not change into click beetles for several years. Then they form pupas in the ground. Late in summer they emerge as beetles.

Blister beetles are black, black and red, reddish-brown, and one kind which eats potato and tomato leaves is yellow and black. They are ½ to ¾ of an inch long. When the beetle is handled, it gives off an oily fluid which irritates the skin.

Adult blister beetles are harmful in the garden, as they eat leaves and flowers. But the grubs of these beetles eat the eggs of grasshoppers and other insects and in that way are helpful. The female lays eggs in the ground which hatch into long-legged creatures. These scurry around until they find some insect eggs. Then they settle down to eat. Soon they become fat creatures without legs. They pass the winter as a grub that is like a pupa. In the spring they become a fat grub again, then a real pupa, then an adult. The adult beetles live only a short time.

Japanese beetles are about ½ inch long and are green with bronze wings. They came to this country from Japan about thirty-five years ago. They have done a great deal of damage to farm and garden crops. Late in summer the female lays eggs in the ground. The grubs which hatch from the eggs eat roots. They live through the winter. In spring they become pupas and in summer, adult beetles. One way to destroy Japanese beetles is to drop them into a can of kerosene.

The Colorado potato beetle, which is now as numerous in the east as it is in the west, is about ½ inch long and almost as wide. It is yellow with ten black stripes down its outer wings. The grubs are red with black spots down the sides. There are two generations of these beetles a year. These potato beetles are very destructive, since both beetles and grubs eat leaves of potato and related plants.

May beetles, or June bugs, are the stout brown beetles, ½ to 1 inch long, which beat against windows on early summer nights. Both the adults and the grubs are harmful to gardens. The beetles eat the leaves and flowers. The grubs are the fat white worms which eat the roots of plants. They live in the ground for two or three years before they become pupas and, later, adult beetles.

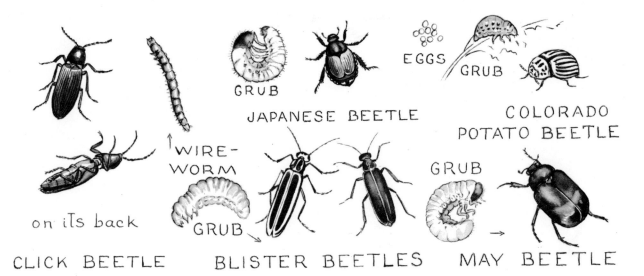

GRUB

JAPANESE BEETLE

EGGS GRUB

COLORADO POTATO BEETLE

on its back

↑WIRE-WORM

GRUB

GRUB

CLICK BEETLE   BLISTER BEETLES   MAY BEETLE

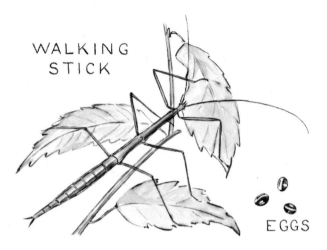

WALKING STICK

EGGS

ODD INSECTS

If you seem to see a twig on a bush suddenly come alive and walk off, you are probably looking at a stick insect, or walking stick. These insects have thin green or brown bodies that are 3 or 4 inches long when they are full grown. They have no wings. They live in bushes and trees and eat the leaves. Unless there are many of them in one place, they do little damage.

In autumn the female stick insects let their eggs drop to the ground. The eggs are shiny black with a white stripe and look like tiny beans. In spring, soon after the first leaves are out, the eggs hatch into small insects. These are like the adults except in size and in their pale color.

The praying mantis is about the same length as the walking stick. Its body is heavier and it has wings. It can turn its small triangular head to look over its shoulder. Its front legs are broad and spiny. It uses them like claws to catch and hold its prey. When it wants to look ferocious, it spreads its wings and rears up on its back legs.

The Carolina mantis, which is a native American species, lives in the south. It has a brownish or green body and green wings. It grows about 2½ inches long. The female lays her eggs on a twig and covers them with a coating of froth.

The Chinese mantis, which has become common in the northeastern states, grows from 3 to 4 inches long. It is green or brown with a green border on its long wings. In autumn the female lays her eggs in a spongy case. The case is about the size and color of an English walnut. It is fastened to a bush or weed stalk, or sometimes to a twig on a tree.

If you can find an egg case you can keep it in a cool place through the winter and watch the young mantises come out in the spring. They pour from the side of the case and hang there for a little while before darting off. Although they are only a little bigger than mosquitoes, they take the same fierce poses that the adults do.

Young mantises eat plant lice and other small insects. A full-grown mantis eats flies, grasshoppers, butterflies, bees, and other insects. So it is useful to have in the garden and should not be destroyed. It will die in autumn, but its eggs will live through the winter.

PRAYING MANTIS

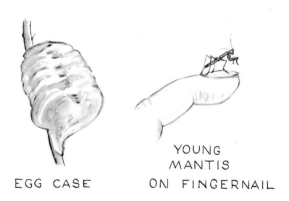

EGG CASE

YOUNG MANTIS ON FINGERNAIL

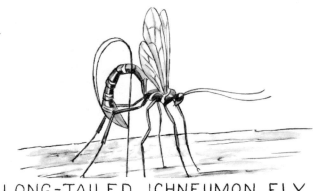

LONG-TAILED ICHNEUMON FLY

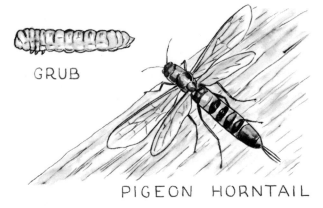

GRUB

PIGEON HORNTAIL

If you have a partly decayed tree in your yard, you may find a rather large insect with a long, slender tail drilling a hole in the bark. This insect is called an ichneumon fly, though it is not a fly but a relative of the wasp. The tail of the female is hardly thicker than a thread, but she is able to bore into wood with it. She selects wood that has horntail grubs in it and lays her eggs in their burrows. When the ichneumon eggs hatch into grubs, they eat the horntail grubs. After they have grown to full size, the ichneumon grubs form pupas and change into adults inside the tree. They gnaw a hole in the wood in order to get out. Since they destroy grubs which damage many kinds of valuable trees, the ichneumon flies are useful insects.

Adult long-tailed ichneumon flies have yellow spotted black or brown bodies about 1¾ inches long. The tail of the female may be 5 inches long.

The pigeon horntail is about 1¾ inches long and is usually yellow with black or brown markings. The female lays her eggs in the wood of a tree, boring into it with her tail. But, since her tail is short, she may get stuck while laying her eggs, and die. The grubs are sometimes found in fire-wood or other wood which is brought into the house.

The golden-eyed lacewing fly is a delicate-looking insect about ⅝ of an inch long, which flies about the garden and comes to lighted windows at night. It has pale green, gauzy wings and brown or golden eyes. If it is handled, it gives off a bad odor. The female lays her eggs on leaves in a curious way. She drops from her tail a bit of fluid and pulls it up into a thread. The thread hardens in the air, and she lays her egg at the top of it. The eggs hatch into tiny grubs which climb down the stems. They eat aphids (plant lice).

In fine soil or sand, sometimes under porches, ant lions, also called doodlebugs, dig little pits in which they catch ants and other small insects. When an insect walks over the edge of the pit, the ant lion sends up a shower of sand to make it tumble down.

The ant lion is the grub of a gauzy-winged insect that looks something like a dragonfly. But it has smaller eyes, and it has antennae (feelers). It folds its wings against its body when it rests. The female drops her eggs into the ground.

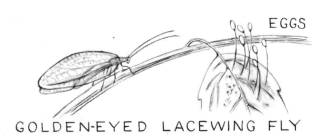

EGGS

GOLDEN-EYED LACEWING FLY

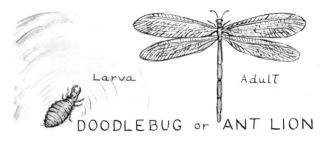

Larva   Adult

DOODLEBUG or ANT LION

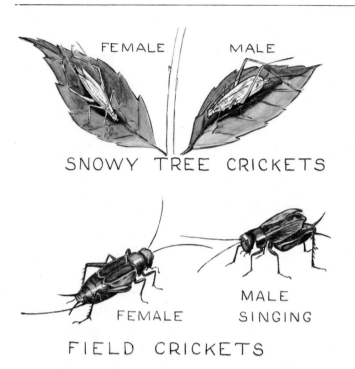

SNOWY TREE CRICKETS

FEMALE   MALE

FIELD CRICKETS

FEMALE   MALE SINGING

Empty shell of nymph after adult has broken out
CICADA

INSECT NOISEMAKERS

On hot summer days and nights you hear many different kinds of noises made by insects.

Tree crickets are slender, pale green insects about ½ inch long, and they have delicate-looking, gauzy wings. It is with them that the tree crickets make the shrill, chirping sound that fills the night air. When they chirp, they raise their wings straight up and flutter them rapidly against each other. The hotter the weather, the faster they chirp.

Female tree crickets lay their eggs in the bark or twigs of trees or bushes. In early summer the eggs hatch into wingless crickets. Tree crickets are useful to have in the garden as they eat aphids (plant lice).

Field crickets sing both day and night. They rasp one wing over the other to make a chirping sound. A file on the inside of one wing scratches against a heavy ridge on the other wing. These crickets live in fields and gardens. They are black and grow to about 1 inch long. The brown cricket, which also lives in fields, is less than ½ inch long. The house cricket is slightly larger. Female crickets lay eggs in holes which they make in the ground with the long spear at the end of their bodies. Some eggs hatch into small crickets which live through the winter. Other eggs do not hatch until spring. Most of the adult crickets die when cold weather comes.

The cicada, or locust, has a wide black body about 1½ inches long. It has red markings if it is the seventeen-year locust, or green markings if it is the two-year kind. Its gauzy wings are longer than its body. It makes a humming sound on hot days in the latter part of summer. This sound is made by a sort of drum on each side of its body, which it vibrates by using muscles in its body. Only the males make a noise. This is also true of the other noise-making insects. The duty of the female is to lay eggs.

Female cicadas lay eggs in twigs of trees late in summer. The eggs hatch into grubs, or nymphs, which fall to the ground and burrow underneath. Some kinds remain in the ground two years. Others stay for thirteen or seventeen years before they come to the surface and split their skins to change into adult locusts.

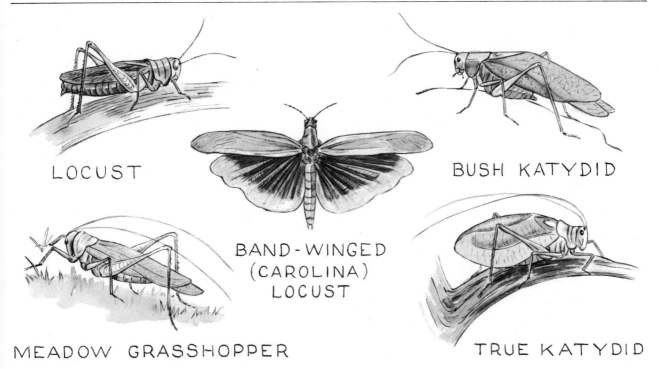

LOCUST

BUSH KATYDID

BAND-WINGED
(CAROLINA)
LOCUST

MEADOW GRASSHOPPER

TRUE KATYDID

There are many different kinds of grasshoppers, but all of them belong to one of two groups. They are either short-horned grasshoppers (locusts), or they are of the long-horned variety which includes the katydids. Among the short-horned kind are the band-winged, or gay-winged, locusts. These have brownish or gray outer wings and under wings of bright yellow, red, or brown with a dark or light band. When the locust flies, the under wings spread out like a fan. The Carolina locust has brown outer wings and dark brown under wings with a light border. It is about 1⅜ inches long. Another kind of short-horned locust, the yellow-striped, has brown, yellow, or blue-green hind legs. The large locusts are about 2 inches long. Another kind, pigmy locusts, are less than ½ inch long.

Most grasshoppers do not live through the winter. In autumn the female locusts drill holes in the ground with the end of their bodies and lay their eggs. In spring the eggs hatch into small wingless locusts.

Meadow grasshoppers belong to the long-horned group. Of the two common kinds, one grows about 2 inches long, including the wings. It is pale green.

The female has a curved end to her body with which she lays eggs in plant tissues. The other common kind is much smaller. It has short wings and very long antennae, or feelers. The female has a long spear at the end of her body through which she lays her eggs. The meadow grasshoppers eat mostly grasses and are not so destructive to garden crops as the locusts are.

Katydids are about 2 inches long and have wings which look like green leaves. The bush katydid lays her eggs in rows on leaves. The true katydid has wider wings than the bush katydid. It lives in trees and eats the leaves. The female lays her eggs in slits in the bark.

Most of the grasshoppers sing in the daytime. The locust fiddles by rubbing its long hind legs against its wings. Some kinds make a crackling sound when they fly, by rattling their hind wings against their front wings. The meadow grasshopper scrapes one wing over the other to make a rasping sound. The bush katydid makes a *zeep* sound in daytime or at night. The true katydid carries on its argument at night. Both kinds sing by scraping one wing over the other.

ADULTS   BUBBLE HOUSE   YOUNG
FROGHOPPER

HOPPING INSECTS

In spring and summer you often see on the stems of plants small masses of froth that look like spittle. If you separate the bubbles, you will find a tiny green insect inside. It is a young froghopper. It is called this because the wide head of the adult insect is somewhat like a frog's. If you touch it, it will jump like a frog.

If you want to see how the young insect makes the froth house in which it lives, put it on another part of the plant stem. It will go to work, giving off a fluid from its body and whipping it into bubbles by rotating its tail end. Why it does this is not known. The froth may be a protection from enemies or it may keep the soft insect from drying out.

After you have watched the froghopper make the froth, put the piece of stem containing it in a glass jar. In a few days you will find a brown bug about ¼ of an inch long in place of the little green one that made the bubbles. The young insect has shed its skin and turned into a winged adult.

Froghoppers suck the juices of stems and leaves. In autumn the female lays her eggs in plant stems. In spring the eggs hatch into the green bubble-making insects.

LEAF HOPPERS

Leaf hoppers are tiny, slender insects that we find on trees, bushes, and in grass. The rose leaf hopper is white or pale green and about ⅛ of an inch long. If there are many of them on a rose bush, they are a serious pest. There are two generations in a summer. The young insects that come in spring hatch from eggs that were laid in autumn. In summer more eggs are laid. The adult insects fly to apple trees and eat their leaves.

Another leaf hopper is a pretty little insect about ¼ of an inch long. It has stripes of red and green on the back and yellow on the head. It is found on garden flowers.

TREE HOPPERS

Tree hoppers are odd insects. They are less than ½ of an inch long. They have such peculiar shapes that they are called insect brownies. It is fun to look at them under a magnifying glass. The buffalo tree hopper is green or yellowish. It has a broad hump on its head end. When it rests on a stem it looks like a bud. Another hopper, when it sits on a stem, looks like a brown thorn. You do not know it is an insect until you see it move. Ants are sometimes seen with it and with some of the other hoppers, since hoppers secrete a honeydew that the ants like. Another brown hopper has two humps, like a camel or a saddle.

Under the oddly shaped hard wings that form the back of the tree hopper are the gauzy wings with which it flies. The adults fly and hop in trees and bushes, where the females lay their eggs. The young hoppers are more often found near the ground, where they suck the juices of plants. The eggs are laid in summer, and the young insects hatch the following spring.

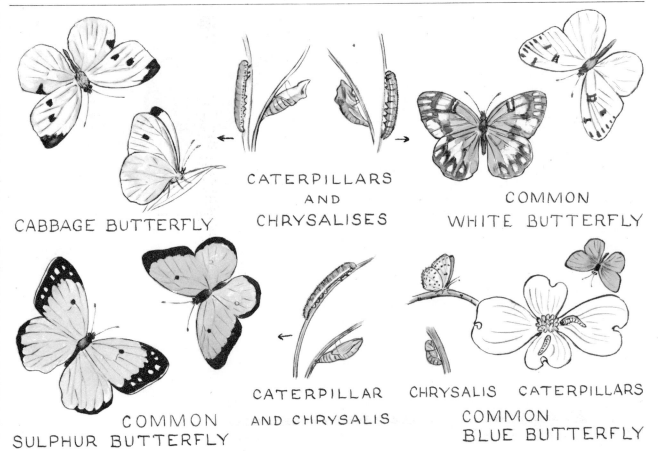

CABBAGE BUTTERFLY

CATERPILLARS
AND
CHRYSALISES

COMMON
WHITE BUTTERFLY

COMMON
SULPHUR BUTTERFLY

CATERPILLAR
AND CHRYSALIS

CHRYSALIS   CATERPILLARS
COMMON
BLUE BUTTERFLY

SMALL BUTTERFLIES

If you have flowers in your yard you will have butterflies and caterpillars. The caterpillars hatch from eggs that the butterflies lay. When they are full grown they make chrysalises and change into butterflies.

One kind that you find everywhere is the cabbage butterfly. Although it came from Europe originally, it is now common all over the United States. Cabbage butterflies are about 2 inches across. They are white with a yellowish tinge on the under side. They have a dark patch at the front corners of the wings, and the females have two dark spots in the fore wing. The caterpillars are green with three yellow stripes. They eat cabbage and other plants of the mustard family and grow to about 1 inch long.

Common sulphur butterflies vary from orange-yellow to pale yellow in color and from 1¼ to 2¼ inches across. They have a dark border on the wings and sometimes dark spots. The caterpillars are small and are green with lighter stripes on the sides. They eat clovers and other plants of the pea family. The chrysalis is pale green.

The common white butterfly is much like the cabbage butterfly, but it has dark spots instead of dark corners on its fore wings. The female is light brown with white and brown spots. The small caterpillar is green and yellow. It eats cabbage and other plants of the mustard family. The chrysalis is small and brownish.

The common blue butterfly and others of the same family are very small. They vary from pale blue to brown on the upper side of the wings. Underneath they are white or light gray with brown specks and brown borders on the wings. One kind of caterpillar is white with a black line and a brown head. Another kind is dark green with a black head. They feed on flowers of dogwood, clover, and other plants. The chrysalises are brownish.

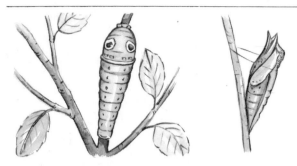

TIGER SWALLOWTAIL CATERPILLAR

This caterpillar grows to about 2 inches long. It is green with two eyespots of blue, yellow, and black. It eats the leaves of wild cherry, birch, poplar, and other trees. When full grown, it changes to a wood-brown chrysalis.

TIGER SWALLOWTAIL

The wings of this butterfly are yellow with black markings. Sometimes the females have dark wings. They are 4 inches or more across.

FRITILLARY CATERPILLAR

This fritillary caterpillar hatches in autumn and lives through the winter. In spring it eats violet leaves. It grows to 1½ inches long and is black with orange-and-black spines. Then it changes into a mottled, dark brown chrysalis.

FRITILLARIES

These butterflies are golden brown with black markings. On the under side they have silver spots. They vary in size from 1½ to 3 inches across.

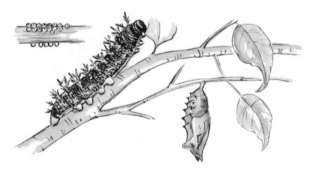

MOURNING CLOAK CATERPILLAR

This caterpillar grows to 2 inches long. It is spiny and is black with white specks and red spots. It eats elm, poplar, willow, and other tree leaves. It forms a brown chrysalis with red tips.

MOURNING CLOAK

This butterfly lives through the winter. It is dark reddish-brown with a yellow border and blue spots. Underneath it is marked like tree bark. It is about 3 inches across.

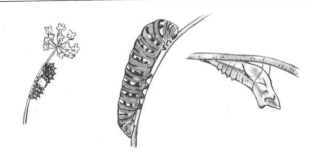

BLACK SWALLOWTAIL CATERPILLAR

The young caterpillar is black with a white band and is spiny. When full grown (nearly 2 inches long) it is smooth and green with black rings and yellow spots. Then it makes a light brown chrysalis.

BLACK or EASTERN SWALLOWTAIL

The wings of this butterfly are black with rows of yellow spots and blue spots on the hind wings. The wing spread is about 3 inches.

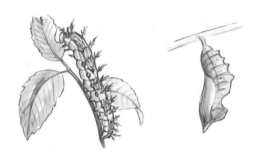

VIOLET-TIP CATERPILLAR

This caterpillar is brown and yellow with dark brown and white stripes and branching spines on the back. It eats elm, hop, and nettle leaves. Then it forms a light brown, irregular chrysalis.

VIOLET-TIP or QUESTION-SIGN

This angle-wing butterfly is reddish-brown with black marks and violet on the edges of its wings. Underneath it is lighter and has a silver mark like a question sign. It is 2½ inches across.

MONARCH CATERPILLAR

The monarch caterpillar eats milkweed leaves. It is ringed with yellow, white, and black. It grows to 2 inches long, then it makes a pale green chrysalis spotted with gold and black.

1) MONARCH or MILKWEED; 2) VICEROY

The wings of both these butterflies are reddish-brown with black lines. The monarch is about 4 inches across; the viceroy is smaller and has an extra black line across the hind wings.

CECROPIA

EGGS

COCOON

CATERPILLAR

GIANT MOTHS

Most of the large moths fly at night. Some live only a short time as they do not eat. A few, like the tomato sphinx, fly at dusk and sip nectar from the flowers.

The cecropia moth has reddish-brown wings with a light brown border. Each wing has a red and a white line and a white crescent spot with a red and black border. The body is dull red with white bands. The male moths are from 4½ to 5 inches across, and the females may be 6 inches across. The females lay eggs on wild cherry, willow, and other trees and shrubs. The caterpillars which hatch from the eggs grow to about 4 inches long. When mature, they are bluish-green with blue, black, yellow, and red warts (tubercles) down the back. They spin large cocoons lengthwise on twigs. The following spring the moths come out.

The large green worm that you find on tomato plants wriggles underground when it is full grown and becomes a pupa with a hard brown case. In spring the pupa works its way out of the ground. Then a moth, the tomato sphinx, with mottled and striped grayish-brown wings breaks out. When fully spread, the wings are 3 or 4 inches across. The body is grayish or brownish with two rows of yellow spots. The tongue, when uncoiled, is longer than the body, and is able to reach into tubular flowers.

Another caterpillar that we often meet in yards and fields is the brown-and-black woolly bear. It hibernates in cold weather and makes a cocoon in spring. The cocoon is woolly like the caterpillar, as its hairs are worked into the silk. The moth (Isabella tiger) that comes out of the cocoon is yellowish-tan with dark specks on its wings and rows of dark spots down its body. It is about 2 inches across the wings.

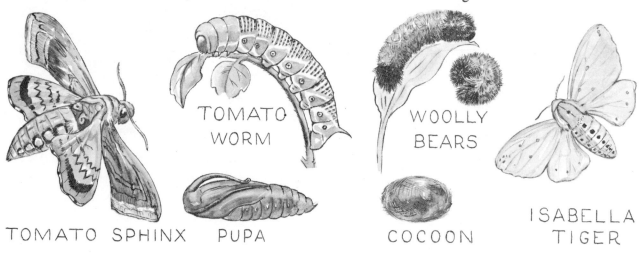

TOMATO WORM

WOOLLY BEARS

TOMATO SPHINX   PUPA

COCOON

ISABELLA TIGER

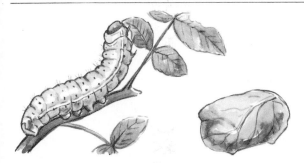

LUNA CATERPILLAR

The luna caterpillar grows to about 3 inches long and is green with a yellow line and red spots along the sides. It eats the leaves of birch, willow, and other trees. The cocoon that it makes between leaves usually falls to the ground.

LUNA

This beautiful, pale green moth has long tails on its hind wings. There is a purple vein on its fore wing. Its body is furry white. The wing spread is from 3½ to 4½ inches.

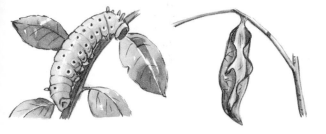

PROMETHEA CATERPILLAR

This caterpillar feeds on spice bush, sassafras, wild cherry, and other trees. It grows to 2 or 3 inches long and has a blue-green body with rows of black tubercles and four red tubercles. Then it spins a slim cocoon inside a hanging leaf.

PROMETHEA

The male promethea moth is dark reddish-brown or black with a tan border. The female is lighter. The wing spread is from 3 to 4 inches.

POLYPHEMUS CATERPILLAR

This caterpillar is green like the leaves of the trees on which it feeds. It has bright orange spots on the sides and grows to about 3 inches long. Then it makes a fat cocoon inside a hanging leaf.

POLYPHEMUS

The tan wings of this moth have a yellow border. Each wing has an eyespot, the ones on the hind wing having a blue and a black border. The wing spread is from 5½ to 6 inches.

DADDY LONGLEGS (HARVESTMAN)

ORB WEB

FUNNEL WEB

GRASS SPIDER

CRAB SPIDERS

SPINY SPIDER

WOLF SPIDER

EGG SAC

HARVESTMEN AND SPIDERS

Harvestmen and spiders are not insects. They have eight legs; insects have six. They lay eggs which hatch into small harvestmen and spiders. There are no grubs or pupas. You can tell the harvestmen, or daddy longlegs, from the spiders by their long thin legs and small rounded bodies.

The daddy longlegs travels over plants, usually in the evening, searching for aphids and other small insects to eat. It uses its second pair of legs, which are longer than the others, for feelers. Its eyes are on a little hump on its back. In autumn the females lay eggs in the earth. Then the adults die. The eggs hatch the next spring.

Crab spiders also catch small insects on plants. They do not spin webs. In spring they usually stay on white or pink flowers. Then the spiders are white with pink marks. Later, when they stay on goldenrod and other yellow flowers, their bodies turn yellow. They are ½ inch or less in length. The female lays her eggs in a silken sac which she fastens to a curled leaf or other support.

The spiny spider is curiously shaped with black thorny points and spots on its hard white abdomen. The under part of the abdomen is striped black and white and comes to a point. It is from the point that the spider spins the silk for its finely woven orb web. After the web is completed, the spider tears out the center and sits there waiting for a passing insect to be caught in it.

The webs of the grass spiders decorate our lawns, especially after a rain or heavy dew. Some of them are funnel-shaped with a hole in the center where the spider hides. When an insect falls into the web, the spider dashes out and captures it. These spiders are from ½ inch or less long to ¾ of an inch. They are yellowish or brown with two black lines on the back. The female lays eggs in a silken sac, or cocoon, which she leaves under the web or some other protection. The adults die in winter and the eggs hatch in spring.

Wolf spiders eat small insects which they chase and catch on the ground. Some of them live in holes in the ground. Sometimes they make a wall of small sticks, held together by silk, around the opening of the hole. These spiders are from ½ to ¾ of an inch long. They are gray or brown with yellow stripes down the back. The female lays eggs in a sac like a tiny football, which she drags after her until the young hatch. Then the baby spiders crawl up on her back and ride around for a while. Soon they are able to care for themselves.

The orange (also called the black-and-yellow) garden spider makes a handsome web that often stretches from supports that are many feet apart. The sticky threads of the web catch insects as large as grasshoppers and bees. The spider's legs are coated with a film of oil which keeps them from sticking to the web. When an insect is caught, the spider runs to it and either eats it at once or wraps it in silk and leaves it hanging on the web.

The female spider grows an inch or more long. She has a velvety-black body with yellow markings. The head section is gray, and the legs are orange and black. The male is brown and white and only ¼ of an inch long. After they mate, the female often eats the male. In autumn she lays many hundreds of tiny yellow eggs in a pear-shaped sac, or cocoon, about the size of a hickory nut. It has a sort of varnish over it for protection. All winter it hangs from a weed stalk or other support. Although the young spiders hatch, they do not leave the sac until the following spring.

The banded garden spider is a little smaller than the orange spider. The female is white with narrow black-and-yellow bands. The male is about 1/5 of an inch long and is yellow and white.

Like its orange relative, the banded spider makes a large orb web which stretches between weeds or trees. The spider may start the framework by floating a silk thread into the air until this sticks to a support. Then it makes the rest of the frame of lines radiating from the center. Starting at the center, it spins a spiral scaffold line of ungummed silk. Then, starting at the outside, it makes a spiral of sticky threads. The spider holds up the silk thread and guides it with a hind leg as it goes along. Below the center of the web it makes a wide spiral band like a ladder.

In autumn the female lays her eggs in a cup-shaped sac, or cocoon, with a flat top. She fastens it to branches or leaves.

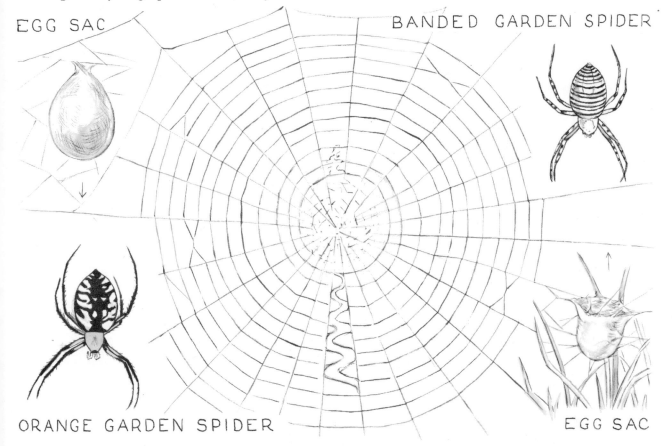

EGG SAC

BANDED GARDEN SPIDER

ORANGE GARDEN SPIDER

EGG SAC

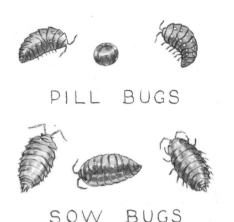

CENTIPEDES AND MILLIPEDES

Under stones and in rotting wood with the pill bugs and sow bugs, you may find centipedes and millipedes. The common centipede has a shiny reddish-brown segmented (ringed) body about 1½ inches long. It has fifteen pairs of legs. Poison in the first pair of legs is used to kill the earthworms and insects which it eats. The female lays eggs on the ground. The eggs are sticky, and she rolls each one over until it is coated with earth.

The centipede that is found in houses has a light-colored body with three dark stripes down the back. It is about 1¼ inches long, but its spidery legs make it seem longer. The young centipedes hatch from eggs. They have seven pairs of legs at first, and more develop later. Although you may not like to see centipedes around the house, they actually are useful as they eat insects, including cockroaches and moths.

Millipedes are long (2½ to 4 inches) wormlike creatures which roll up when they are disturbed. They do not have the thousand legs that their name means, but they do have a great many. There are two pairs of legs to each segment, where the centipede has one pair. When they first hatch from eggs, they may have only three pairs of legs. As they grow and molt, the number increases to thirty pairs or more. Millipedes are found in dark, moist places like rotting logs or piles of dead leaves. They eat plant rather than animal matter and they usually feed on decaying wood or leaves. It is only when they eat the roots of plants that they do any harm in the garden. In winter they curl up and hibernate.

PILL BUGS AND SOW BUGS

If you turn over a large flat stone in your yard you will probably raise the roof that shelters many small creatures. Among them you will be likely to find pill bugs and sow bugs. They are small, hard-shelled creatures about ½ inch long and are dark grayish or mottled brown in color. Some are spotted with white.

Pill bugs roll up in tight balls when you touch them. Sow bugs cannot roll up so tightly. Both live under rocks where the soil is moist and in rotting wood. They are sometimes called wood lice. They eat decaying wood and leaves, and growing plants, but they do not usually harm the garden. The female pill bugs and sow bugs carry their eggs under their bodies. For a short time after the eggs hatch, they carry the young ones. These are like the parents except in size.

Pill bugs and sow bugs are not insects. They have crustlike shells and so are crustaceans, like lobsters and crabs.

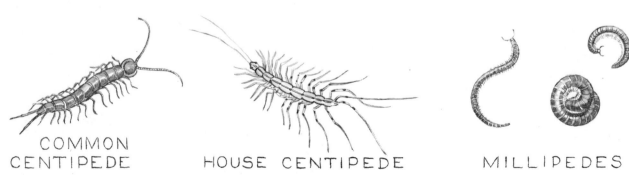

COMMON CENTIPEDE   HOUSE CENTIPEDE   MILLIPEDES

SHELLS OF
STRIPED
WOOD SNAIL

WHITE-LIPPED SNAIL

SHELLS OF
AMBER SNAIL

SNAILS AND SLUGS

We often find snails and slugs in our gardens. They have soft, slimy bodies which draw together and spread out as they move along. Usually they leave a trail of slime behind them. The head end of the body has two pairs of stalks, or tentacles, and the eyes are on the end of the longer stalks. Inside its mouth the snail (and the slug) has a tongue, or radula, which has rows of teeth on it. By working the tongue back and forth like a file, the snail or slug breaks up the food that it eats. Snails have spiral shells on their backs. Slugs do not have any shells that you can see.

Every snail and slug is both male and female and is able to lay eggs after mating. The eggs are usually laid in small masses in damp places like the under side of stones or decaying leaves. The eggs that are laid in spring and summer hatch into tiny snails or slugs in two or three weeks. The eggs laid in autumn may not hatch until the following spring. In winter snails seal themselves up in their shells. Slugs curl up and hibernate in the ground or under stones or leaves.

Snails and slugs eat growing plants and other vegetable or animal matter. They are usually more active at night. If they attack your garden put ashes around the plants. Or put some Paris green on cabbage or lettuce leaves scattered on the ground.

The striped wood snail has brown markings on a light shell that is a little over ½ inch across when it is full size.

The white-lipped snail has a fairly large shell (1¼ or more inches across). It is pale brown or pinkish and has a white border, or lip, around the opening.

The amber snail has an oval-shaped yellowish or reddish-brown shell about ½ inch long. It is too small to cover the body entirely when the snail tries to draw itself into its shell.

The field slug grows to 1½ or more inches long. Its color varies from yellowish to dark brown. The small opening on the right side of the high part of the back is the place through which it breathes.

The garden slug is 1½ inches long and is light gray with a dark line along the sides.

The large black slug that is often seen in gardens and greenhouses came from Europe. It grows from 4 to 6 inches long and is slimy yellowish or grayish-white with rows of black spots or lines down its back.

Eggs Young

FIELD SLUG

GARDEN SLUG

Eggs

BLACK SLUG

GARTER SNAKE

GARTER SNAKE

This snake is often found in yards and gardens. There are several varieties in the United States and Canada. The common garter snake grows to about 3 feet long. It has one light-colored and two dark brown stripes down its back. Underneath it is light. Ribbon snakes look somewhat like garter snakes, but they are smaller, brighter in color, and more likely to be found near water.

Garter snakes are not poisonous, but they will bite and give off a bad odor if annoyed. When caught and tamed they may be fed earthworms and small fish. Their usual food is frogs, toads, salamanders, earthworms, and insects. Early in spring garter snakes come out of hibernation. They mate and in late summer the young are born. A female may have from twelve to seventy young ones, each about 6 inches long.

BLACK SNAKE

BLACK SNAKE

Another rather common snake around houses is the black snake. It is black on the back and dark gray underneath. Its chin and throat are white. When full grown these snakes are 6 feet long. They are not poisonous, but they can bite severely. The young snakes are gray with dark blotches. They hatch in summer from eggs which are laid in June or July. Each female snake lays from five to twenty white, tough-shelled eggs.

Black snakes can crawl up bushes and trees. You may have seen them getting into birds' nests. Young birds and eggs are only a small part of their food. Black snakes also eat mice, rats, small snakes, frogs, and insects.

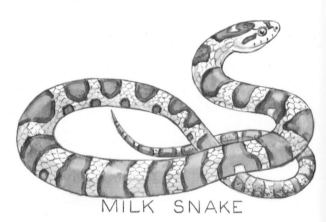

MILK SNAKE

MILK SNAKE

The milk snake is gray on the back with a row of dark patches. Underneath it is light, checkered with dark spots. It grows to 40 inches long. In summer the female snake lays small batches of leathery white eggs, which she buries in the ground or in rotting wood. In September snakes 6 to 8 inches long hatch from the eggs.

Milk snakes live chiefly on mice and rats, which they often catch around barns. This gave farmers the idea that the snakes milked the cows. That is not true, but the snakes are still called milk snakes. They are harmless and make good pets. Milk snakes should not be mistaken for copperheads, which have wider heads and differently shaped patches on their backs.

HOG-NOSED SNAKE

HOG-NOSED SNAKE or PUFF ADDER

This snake is a good bluffer. It may look dangerous, but it really is not. It grows to 3½ feet long and has a thick body which is yellowish-brown or reddish-brown with many dark patches. Underneath it is yellowish with dark marks on the sides. It has a turned-up snout.

If the snake is startled it will flatten out its head and neck and puff out its body by taking a deep breath. Then it lets the breath out with a loud, hissing sound. It may also give off bad-smelling matter. If none of these actions drive off the enemy it will play dead and remain limp for some time.

In summer the female snake lays from twenty-four to thirty-six eggs in damp soil. The young, which are 6½ to 8 inches long, hatch before cold weather. Then they all hibernate. The young snakes eat insects. The adult snakes eat chiefly frogs and toads.

GREEN or GRASS SNAKE

The green, or grass, snake grows to 20 inches in length. Its back is bright green; underneath it is lighter colored. The female lays small batches of eggs, usually under stones, in August. Green snakes are harmless. They are useful in the garden as they eat many insects.

COPPERHEAD

The copperhead is the only poisonous snake pictured on these pages. Copperhead poison is very dangerous. Anyone who gets bitten by this snake should have help at once.

The copperhead is usually found in woods, fields, and swamps, but it might stray into a back yard. It grows to 40 inches long and to 1½ inches across. It is light brown with widely spaced markings of reddish-brown. The marks are narrow in the middle and wider at the sides. Underneath, the snake is a light-pinkish color with two rows of dark spots. The head is broad at the base where it joins the neck. You can tell this snake from other brownish snakes by its wide head and by the shape of the dark marks on its back. The young snakes have bright yellow tips to their tails. The female has from six to nine young, which are born alive in late summer or early autumn.

Copperheads eat frogs, small birds, small snakes, and mice.

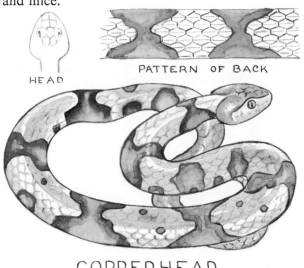

HEAD

PATTERN OF BACK

COPPERHEAD

GREEN SNAKE

TURTLES

Turtles usually live in ponds and woods. Sometimes the kinds that live on land, like the box and wood turtles, stray into our yards.

The shell which covers the turtle's back is made from its ribs and backbone grown together. The upper part of the shell is the carapace; the under part, which covers the stomach, is the plastron. The two parts are joined together at the sides. When attacked by an enemy, the turtle draws its body inside the shell. The box turtle has a hinged plastron which it can pull tightly against the carapace to seal itself in completely — unless its body has grown too fat to fit inside!

Turtles eat tender leaves, berries, mushrooms, earthworms, insects, snails, slugs, small shellfish, and small fish. A pet turtle may be fed raw beef, fish, lettuce, and earthworms. Turtles have no teeth to chew with. They tear their food apart with their front claws and break it up with the sharp edges of their jaws. A turtle can go for some time without eating.

Early in summer the females lay their eggs on the ground. After covering the eggs they leave them to hatch by themselves. The wood turtle buries her eggs, from two to twelve of them, in the sand. The box turtle lays from three to eight eggs in a hole in the ground. They hatch in three months. It takes young turtles four years to grow up and they may live for sixty years or longer.

In winter the wood turtle hibernates under water. Some box turtles do also, but most of them go underground. In autumn the box turtle starts digging in the ground. It gradually works down to a depth of about 2 feet, and there it sleeps until spring.

The box turtle has an arched upper shell, which is brown with yellow spots. It has light spots on the head and neck. The male has red eyes. The female has brown or yellow eyes. When full grown, these turtles are 5 or 6 inches long.

Wood turtles have a brown upper shell with yellow and black markings. The under shell is yellow with black blotches. The upper shell is divided into sections which are slightly raised and marked with lines and ridges. This makes the shell look as if it had been carved. These turtles grow to 6½ inches or longer.

BOX TURTLE   WOOD TURTLE

AMERICAN TOAD

TOADS AND FROGS

Toads often live in our gardens. During the heat of the day they usually hide under buildings or in other shady spots. Late in the afternoon they hunt for insects, snails, and slugs. These they catch with a quick thrust of their long, sticky tongues. Because of what they eat, you can see they are useful creatures to have around.

Toads are not poisonous to people. They secrete a fluid in the two large warts back of their eyes. This fluid is irritating to the mouth of any animal that attempts to bite them.

In spring toads, like frogs, journey to ponds or other bodies of water. The male toad bulges his throat out like a little balloon and sings to attract a mate. The female is much larger than the male — about 5 inches long to his 3 inches. She lays her eggs in the water in long strings of jelly. Each female lays thousands of eggs, many of which are eaten by fish and other creatures. In a few days, if the weather is warm, the eggs develop into tadpoles. The tadpoles live in the water and eat plants until summer. Then they change into tiny toads. It takes three or four years for them to mature.

Before winter comes, toads burrow into soft earth to a depth of 3 or 4 inches. There they hibernate until spring.

TOAD EGGS

TREE FROG

The tree frog, which is also called tree toad, is a small frog about 2 inches long. It lives in trees in summer. Its color varies from green to gray or brown and it has an irregular dark patch on the upper part of the back. It is hard to see a tree frog, but we often hear them singing at dusk in warm weather.

In spring, usually in May, these frogs go to ponds and swamps. There the males sing to their mates. The females lay jelly-coated eggs, either singly or in small bunches, on the surface of the water. In a few days the eggs hatch into tiny tadpoles with orange tails. Before mid-July the tadpoles change into frogs and leave the water.

Tree frogs eat spiders, flies, aphids, and other small insects. In winter they hibernate in a hollow tree or among the tree roots.

If you live near the woods a wood frog might hop into your garden. It lives on land except in March when the female lays her black-and-white eggs in water. This frog is light brown or dark brown and has a black patch below its eye. The male grows to a little over 2 inches long and the female to 2½ inches. Wood frogs eat insects and earthworms. In winter they hibernate under rocks or other shelter.

TADPOLES   WOOD FROG

MICE

Most of us have had a house mouse in our home at some time. This mouse is not native to America, but it is common everywhere. Probably the first house mice came from Europe with the early settlers. Mice increase in numbers very rapidly. One female may have eight or more families in a year, with four to eight in each. She may have her first family when she is about two months old and she may live four years.

House mice will eat any kind of food that they can find in a house. Some of these mice live in the fields, where they eat seeds and grain. They also eat grain which they find in storehouses. Besides destroying food, mice cause trouble by carrying diseases.

The house mouse has a long hairless tail and dull gray coloring underneath as well as on the back. Its body is about 3½ inches long, and so is its tail.

The white-footed mouse is a little larger than the house mouse, though some of its close relatives are smaller. Its soft fur is gray on the back and white underneath, and its tail is hairy. It has large eyes and ears. It lives in the fields and woods and sometimes comes into houses in autumn. It does not hibernate. In winter it either eats the nuts and grains that it has stored near its nest or it goes out hunting. Sometimes it runs through tunnels in the snow.

White-footed mice make their nests in many different places. Sometimes they use hollow logs on the ground. Sometimes they live in hollows in trees, since they are able to climb. They also take over birds' and squirrels' deserted nests, remodeling them and lining them with grass or soft plant down. There may be young ones in the nest any time from March until October in the northern states, and through most of the year in the south. The female has her first family when she is about eight weeks old. There are from one to nine young mice in a family. These mice eat seeds, berries, and insects.

The meadow mouse is stouter than either the house mouse or the white-footed mouse. It has a short tail, small eyes and ears, and a blunt face. Its rather long, soft fur is brownish-gray. In warm weather it lives in tunnels that it makes in the earth or in trails through grass roots. In winter it burrows through the snow. Its nest is in its tunnel or in a clump of grass. It is lined with plant down or moss. There are from five to nine young ones in each family. As many as thirteen families may be raised during the year. The young grow up fast, and the females have their first families when they are one month old. At the end of their first year the mice are about ready to die of old age — if they have not already been eaten by one of their many enemies!

Meadow mice hunt for food day and night in all kinds of weather. They eat seeds, leaves, tender stems and bark, roots and bulbs. They also eat the farmer's hay and they damage orchards and vegetable and flower gardens.

HOUSE MOUSE   WHITE-FOOTED MOUSE   MEADOW MOUSE

MOLES AND SHREWS

The long ridges of raised earth and grass that you sometimes find in your lawn are made by moles. Gardeners often set traps along the mole hills to catch these small animals. But except to make the ground uneven and to loosen some roots, the mole really does little damage. Its food consists mostly of insects and grubs, so it does as much good as harm. Roots and bulbs are eaten by the meadow mice which run through the mole's tunnels.

The common mole is the size of a large meadow mouse. It, too, has a stout body and a short tail. Its dark gray fur is shorter and finer than that of the mouse, and its front feet are broader and stronger. It has a pointed snout and small eyes and ears so hidden in its fur that you cannot see them. But moles can hear fairly well and can see well enough to tell light from dark. The mole depends on its sensitive nose to guide it through its tunnels and to find its food.

The mole digs its tunnels by pushing the earth to one side with its wide front feet. It has two kinds of tunnels — a deep one that is 1 or 2 feet underground and one just under the surface. There the mole finds worms and insects to eat. It spends most of the winter in the deep tunnel. In spring it has a nest there. Moles have only one family a year. In April four or five baby moles are born. By the end of May they are able to take care of themselves.

Shrews may be in your yard without your knowing it. They run about under the cover of leaves and sometimes use the moles' tunnels. If you have a cat, it may catch more shrews than mice.

Shrews look like small moles except that they have delicate, mouselike feet. They have soft, dark gray or brownish fur and pointed snouts. Their eyes and ears, like the moles', are hidden in their fur. The short-tailed shrew grows to 5 inches long, including its 1-inch tail. It has velvety, dark gray fur. The common shrew is brownish on the back and lighter underneath. It is 4 inches long, with a 1½ inch tail. The pigmy shrew is our smallest mammal. It is about 3 or 4 inches long, with a short tail, and weighs about 1/12 of an ounce.

Shrews have two or three families a year. The babies, usually six or seven of them, are born in a covered nest of leaves and grass. This is made in a hollow log or shallow underground burrow. At first baby shrews are the size of small bees. When they are a month old they are half grown and able to take care of themselves. They are mature at six months; by sixteen months, as a result of their nervous, active life, they are old.

Shrews hunt both day and night in all kinds of weather. They eat insects, worms, snails, salamanders and other small animals including young mice. They sometimes eat a little grain and nuts too. In a day a shrew will eat more than three times its own weight. The bite of a shrew, especially the short-tailed kind, is poisonous.

These little animals eat hardly any vegetable matter and they destroy many insects and other pests. This makes them useful in a garden.

COMMON MOLE   SHORT-TAILED
                         SHREW   COMMON
                                         SHREW

GRAY SQUIRRELS

Gray squirrels are interesting and amusing to watch, though sometimes they are so numerous and so friendly that they become a nuisance. If they get into a house they will chew up anything that they consider suitable for nesting material. But they do not often make their nests in houses; they usually make them in trees.

The winter nest of the gray squirrel is in the hollow of a tree. The summer nest is built in a fork in the tree branches. It is a ball of leaves lined with bits of bark, moss, and fine grass. The squirrels enter the leaf nest through a doorway in its side.

Early in spring the first squirrel family is born, usually in the hollow-tree home. Later in the summer there is another family. There are from two to six young squirrels in each family. They are born blind and without fur. In a few days their fur begins to grow, but they do not open their eyes until they are five weeks old. They stay with the mother squirrel for two months or longer. If she wants to move one of them, she picks it up by the fur of its stomach and it wraps itself around her neck. After the young ones leave the mother they make nests of their own.

In spring the squirrels eat the buds and seeds of maple and other trees. They also eat birds' eggs and young birds. In autumn they eat acorns, beech, hickory, and other nuts. They store many of the nuts in holes in the ground. All through the winter, in mild weather, they come out to dig up the buried nuts. Sometimes the nuts the squirrels forget grow into trees.

These squirrels are gray on the upper parts (sometimes brown on the back) and white or light gray underneath. The gray squirrel grows to about 9 inches long, with a bushy tail as long as its body. Occasionally you may see a squirrel which is all black, and in a few places in the United States there are squirrels which are all white.

RED SQUIRRELS

Red squirrels are smaller than the gray ones. They are 8 inches long, with a 4½-inch tail. They are brownish-red on the upper parts and white underneath, and are brightly colored in summer.

Although smaller than the gray squirrels, the red squirrels are more quarrelsome and usually drive the gray ones away. They chatter and scold at intruders and seldom become tame. They are the enemies of birds, as they eat eggs and young birds.

Red squirrels have one or two families a year, each with from three to six young. The nest is made of leaves, pine needles, moss, bark, or other material. It is built in a hollow tree or sometimes in a burrow in the ground. The young ones open their eyes when they are about four weeks old. They usually stay with the mother squirrel through the summer.

Red squirrels are seen in the woods more often than around houses, as their food consists of seeds from pine and other cones, nuts, mushrooms, and fruit. They hide food under trees, stones, or other places, so they will have plenty to eat in winter.

CHIPMUNKS

These little animals, relatives of the red squirrel, are 6 inches long, with a 3½-inch tail. They are reddish-brown on the back with black and white stripes on the sides. Underneath they are light tan. In their cheek pouches they can carry nuts and seeds. Their cheeks bulge as they scamper off to add to the food supply in their burrows.

Chipmunks can be a nuisance in the garden. They eat bulbs, grain, seeds, and all kinds of berries. But they also eat beetles, slugs, cutworms, and other garden pests.

The chipmunk's home is underground. It has one or more rooms with small tunnels leading to the surface. In one of the rooms the chipmunk stores food for the winter. In another, it sleeps through most of the winter. In spring the mother chipmunk raises from two to six young ones. At first they are blind and without fur. When they are about a month old they open their eyes. By then their fur has grown. They stay with the mother chipmunk for about three months. Then she may raise another family.

Chipmunks often become amusing pets.

LITTLE BROWN BAT

RED BAT

BIG BROWN BAT

BATS

Bats sometimes get into buildings, as they are able to crawl through cracks. You may have seen one in your house or yard, or darting about in the air at dusk. Bats are the only mammals which are able to fly. A fold of skin stretches between the long bones of their fingers and is attached to the body, forming wings. Bats catch insects in their mouths while flying. These are the only food they eat. The hours just after sunset and before sunrise are when bats do most of their hunting for insects. When bats are thirsty, they fly close to a body of water and scoop up a drink.

While flying, the bats send out high-pitched cries which we cannot hear. These cries echo back to the bat when it comes near an object. In this way it is able to guide its course and avoid bumping into anything in the dark. It is very unlikely that a bat would ever get tangled in a person's hair, as people used to think. Nor is it true to say, "blind as a bat." Bats' small, bright eyes are able to see, even in sunlight.

After it eats, the bat often returns to its resting place and hangs itself up to sleep until it gets hungry again. It usually hangs by its feet with its head down. The sharp curved claws on its toes can hook onto small cracks. They also help the bat to crawl and climb.

In May, June, or July, mother bats have from one to four young ones. The baby bats are born blind and without fur. At first the mother bat carries them along when she flies and holds them folded in her wings when she rests. When the young ones are two weeks old or less, they are half grown. Then they are too big to be carried around. They cling to the roost when the mother is away. About a week later they begin to fly, and soon they are able to catch their own food.

In winter some kinds of bats migrate to warmer climates. Some hang themselves up in caves or other sheltered places to hibernate.

The red bat has orange-red fur and is about 4 inches long.

The little brown bat is grayish-brown and a little over 3½ inches long.

The big brown bat, which often lives around houses, is about 5½ inches long.

The smallest kind of bat is the pipistrelle. Its body is about 2 inches long and it has yellow-brown fur.

COTTONTAIL RABBIT

This animal is a frequent and unwelcome visitor in flower and vegetable gardens. As its food consists entirely of plants, it may do considerable damage. In winter it eats the bark of trees, often doing harm to orchards.

If you can manage to fence it out of the garden, you may enjoy having a cottontail around. It is a pretty animal with its neat fur coat, dark brown on the back and white underneath. Its white tail is conspicuous when it hops on its long legs.

Rabbits have many enemies, including man. They would not be so numerous if they did not have several families during the year. One female may have four sets of from four to seven young ones between February and October. The babies grow up fast. In about a week they open their eyes. After two weeks they leave their fur-lined nest in the grass and hop about, finding tender leaves to eat.

During the day the rabbit rests in a little hollow in the grass or under shrubs or trees. It comes out to feed early in the evening. In winter it finds shelter in a hollow log or cave.

WOODCHUCK

Another animal that you may find eating your vegetables is the woodchuck. It has coarse, grayish-brown fur and weighs from five to twelve pounds. Its home is an underground burrow in the fields. It makes this at the end of a tunnel which is several feet long. The woodchuck digs with its front feet and places the soil around the main opening. There are other tunnels leading from the burrow, with openings in the grass. The woodchuck can escape through them if necessary.

Woodchucks seldom stray far from home, even to find food. This is chiefly plants, though it may include a few insects and mice. Woodchucks feed in early morning and in late afternoon and evening.

In spring from two to six young ones are born in the burrow. At first they are blind and without fur. When they are four weeks old they open their eyes. Soon after that they play outside and eat green plants. By the end of summer they find homes of their own.

Early in fall the woodchuck enters its burrow. There it rolls itself up into a ball to sleep through the winter.

COTTONTAIL RABBIT   WOODCHUCK

OPOSSUMS

SKUNKS

OPOSSUM

Most opossums live in the southern states, though some are found as far north as Vermont. Their home is in the woods, but occasionally one strays into a back yard, even in or near a big city.

An opossum is about the size of a cat and weighs from 8 to 15 pounds. Its long, coarse fur is grayish on the back and light yellow on the head. Its long, naked tail is used to help in climbing trees. The young ones ride on their mother's back, curling their tails around hers or clinging to her fur.

In the south the first family is born in January or February; the second, in May or June. In the north only one family is raised — in spring. There are twelve or more young ones in a family, but usually all do not live to grow up. The babies are tiny — smaller than bumblebees — and are only partly developed when they are born. They stay in the mother's pouch for two months or more.

Opossums eat meat, eggs, insects, fruit, and grain. Their enemies include men who hunt them for food and for their fur. Opossums may fight if cornered, but their usual defense is to play dead.

SKUNK

A young skunk which has been deodorized makes a gentle and affectionate pet. Skunks are born in spring, four to eight of them. Their nest is a pile of dry grass and leaves in an underground den, a hollow log, a cave, or under a house.

At first they are without fur and are blind, but their fur soon grows and after three weeks they open their eyes. In summer the father joins the family, and they all go out hunting at night. Their food consists of insects, some young birds, eggs, mice and other small animals, fruit and berries.

The skunk's defense is the bad-smelling liquid which it squirts from under its tail at anything that attacks it. This is why most other animals leave it alone.

A skunk is about the size of a stout cat. It has a small head, short legs, and a large, bushy tail. The long fur is black with white on the back and tail.

RACCOON

The raccoon's home is in a hollow tree or a den in the rocks, usually near water. If you live near the woods a raccoon may come into your yard, looking for something to eat. Fruit, berries, corn, and grain are among its favorite foods. In the woods it finds and eats insects, bird and turtle eggs, mice, berries and fruit. In the water it catches and eats frogs and fish. If possible, raccoons will wash their food, even a frog or a fish, before eating it.

The raccoon uses its front paws like hands. If you should have one for a pet, you will find that it can open the doors of a room and of a refrigerator. They are likely to get into a lot of mischief in a house! A raccoon must be caught young to make a good pet; older animals are likely to be cranky.

Young raccoons are born in spring, with from two to six in a family. When they are about three weeks old they open their eyes. By the time they are two months old they go hunting with their mother. The family usually stays together through the first winter. Raccoons are full grown when they are two years old. Then they weigh from 15 to 25 pounds. They are gray, brown, and black. They have a black mask across the face and black rings around the tail.

This book will introduce you to the living things that you may find around your home. Other wild animals besides the ones described here may stray into your yard. And you will probably find other birds, other butterflies, other insects, and other plants.

You can learn more about all these creatures and growing things by watching them, and by reading some of the books listed on page 72. The more you know about them, the more you will enjoy your yard and garden.

INDEX

MORE TO READ

BIRDS

Audubon Bird Guide, by Richard H. Pough (Doubleday)
Birds in Their Homes, by Addison Webb (Garden City)
Birds in Your Back Yard, by Ted Pettit (Harper)
Field Book of Eastern Birds, by Leon A. Hausman (Putnam)
Field Guide to the Birds, by Roger Tory Peterson (Houghton; also a Mentor book)
Land Birds East of the Rockies, by Chester A. Reed (Doubleday)

BUTTERFLIES AND MOTHS

American Butterflies and Moths, by Cecile Hulse Matschat (Random House)
Butterfly Book, by W. J. Holland (Doubleday)
Field Guide to the Butterflies of North America, by Alexander B. Klots (Houghton)

FLOWERS

Better Homes and Gardens Garden Book (Meredith)
Field Book of American Wild Flowers, by F. Schuyler Mathews (Putnam)
Gardening, by J. H. Everett (Fawcett)
How to Know the Wild Flowers, by Alfred Stefferud (Holt; also a Mentor book)

SNAKES AND TURTLES, TOADS AND FROGS

Field Book of Snakes of North America and Canada, by Karl P. Schmidt and D. Dwight Davis (Putnam)
First Book of Snakes, by John Hoke (Watts)
Handbook of Frogs and Toads, by Anna A. and Albert H. Wright (Comstock)
They Hop and They Crawl, by Percy A. Morris (Ronald)
Turtles of the United States and Canada, by Clifford H. Pope (Knopf)

INSECTS AND SPIDERS
See also BUTTERFLIES AND MOTHS

Boy's Book of Insects, by Edwin Way Teale (Dutton)
Field Book of Insects, by Frank E. Lutz (Dutton)
First Book of Bugs, by Margaret Williamson (Watts)
Insect Guide, by Ralph B. Swain (Doubleday)
Spider Book, by John Henry Comstock (Comstock)

MAMMALS

Animal Book: American Mammals North of Mexico, by Dorothy and Nils Hogner (Oxford)
Animals of the World, by H. E. Anthony (Garden City)
Mammals of Eastern United States, by William J. Hamilton, Jr. (Comstock)
Meeting the Mammals, by Victor H. Cahalane (Macmillan)

TREES AND SHRUBS

Book of Shrubs, by Alfred Hottes (Dodd)
Fieldbook of American Trees and Shrubs, by F. Schuyler Mathews (Putnam)
First Book of Trees, by M. B. Cormack (Watts)
Handbook of Trees of the Northern States and Canada, by Romeyn Beck Hough (Macmillan)
Our Trees: How to Know Them, by A. I. Emerson and Clarence M. Weed (Garden City)

VEGETABLES AND EDIBLE WILD PLANTS

Burpee's Seed Catalogue (Burpee, Philadelphia)
Edible Wild Plants, by O. P. Medsger (Macmillan)
How to Grow Vegetables, by Lloyd C. Cosper and Harry B. Logan (Duell, Sloan & Pearce)

GENERAL

Fieldbook of Natural History, by E. Lawrence Palmer (McGraw Hill)
Grassroot Jungles, by Edwin Way Teale (Dodd)
In Woods and Fields, by Margaret W. Buck (Abingdon)

NATURE BULLETINS

The National Audubon Society, 1000 Fifth Ave., New York City, publishes many nature bulletins at ten cents each.
Many states also have free or inexpensive publications on trees, shrubs, flowers, birds, mammals, reptiles, and insects. You can write to your state museum, state conservation department, or state department of education at your state capital, for a list of their nature publications.

MAGAZINES

Audubon Magazine, published by National Audubon Society, New York City
Junior Natural History, published by American Museum of Natural History, New York City
National Geographic Magazine, published by National Geographic Society, Washington, D. C.
Natural History, published by American Museum of Natural History, New York City
Nature Magazine, published by American Nature Association, Washington, D. C.
Outdoor Illustrated, published by National Audubon Society, New York City